Ho

PENGUIN AFRICA LIBRARY AP7

Edited by Ronald Segal

Modern Poetry from Africa

D1147921

Modern Poetry from Africa

EDITED BY GERALD MOORE
AND ULLI BEIER

New edition, revised and enlarged

Penguin Books

Penguin Books Ltd, Harmondsworth, Middlesex, England
Penguin Books Inc., 7110 Ambassador Road,
Baltimore, Maryland 21207, U.S.A.
Penguin Books Australia Ltd, Ringwood Victoria, Australia

This selection first published 1963
Reprinted 1965, 1966

This collection copyright © Gerald Moore and Ulli Beier, 1963

Made and printed in Great Britain by
Cox & Wyman Ltd,
London, Fakenham and Reading
Set in Monotype Plantin

Contents

Acknowledgements

For permission to republish the poems in this anthology acknowledgement is made to the poets themselves and to the following copyright holders:

For Jawa Apronti to *Transition*: for Awoonor-Williams to Mbari Publications and *Okyeame*, Accra; for Joseph Bognini to Présence Africaine; for Antoine Roger Bolamba to Présence Africaine; for Emmanuel Boundzeki-Dongala to Présence Africaine; for Kwesi Brew to *Okyeame*; for Dennis Brutus to Mbari Publications; for John Pepper Clark to *Black Orpheus*, Longmans, Mbari Publications and African Universities Press; for José Craveirinha to Pierre-Jean Oswald, Paris; for Noemia De Sousa to Pierre-Jean Oswald; for Birago Diop to Présence Africaine; for David Diop to Présence Africaine; for Mbella Sonne Dipoko to *Transition*; for Michael Echeruo to *Black Orpheus*; for Romanus Egudu to *Black Orpheus*; for Aguinaldo Fonseca to Pierre-Jean Oswald; for Aig Higo to *Transition*; for Antonio Jacinto to Pierre-Jean Oswald; for Patrice Kayo to Présence Africaine; for William Kgositsile to *Transition*; for Ellis Ayitey Komey to *Black Orpheus*; for Valente Malangatana to *Black Orpheus*; for Pol N Ndu to *Black Orpheus*; for Agostinho Neto to *Black Orpheus* and Pierre-Jean Oswald; for Charles Nokan to Présence Africaine; for Gabriel Okara to *Black Orpheus* and African Universities Press, Lagos; for Christopher Okigbo to *Black Orpheus*, Mbari Publications and African Universities Press; for Emile Ologoudou to Présence Africaine; for Lenrie Peters to *Black Orpheus* and Mbari Publications; for Jean-Joseph Rabéarivelo and Flavien Ranaivo to Presses Universitaires de France; for Aldo do Espirito Santo to Pierre-Jean Oswald; for Léopold Sédar Senghor to Éditions du Seuil, Paris and *Black Orpheus*; for Wole Soyinka to Methuen, *Encounter*, *Black Orpheus* and African Universities Press, Lagos; for Tchicaya U Tam'si to Caractères and Pierre-Jean Oswald; for Okogbule Wonodi to Mbari Publications and *Black Orpheus*; for Ouologuem Yambo to Présence Africaine.

Introduction

LEWIS NKOSI, the South African journalist, wrote in the *Observer*, 'Black consciousness really begins with the shock of discovery that one is not only black but is also *non-white*.' The resonance of this remark extends in many directions and will find its peculiar echoes in many situations. The black South African makes this discovery through being utterly rejected by a hostile white-dominated society. But his particular plight, tragic enough in itself, is not of much significance so far as the origin of the following poems is concerned. The discovery may, however, be made in utterly different circumstances. The French African made it precisely because of his *acceptance* – on certain terms – by a metropolitan white society. This society was quite prepared to forgive him his colour just so long as he would clothe it decently in the culture, religion, and manners of a Western civilization. The effect of this approach was to force upon him a reappraisal of what it meant to be a *non-white* in such a situation. Had his colour really no more significance than this? Was he not, after all, rather a black man existing in his own rich if ruined world than a non-white entering on sufferance into another?

Thus the effect of the policy of *assimilation* was to turn the attention of the *assimilé* back upon the one factor which the colonizer wanted him to forget – his blackness. Smothered by the paternal embrace of metropolitan culture, he escaped from it to examine his own with fresh eyes and new understanding.

This gesture, simultaneously one of rejection and

assertion, was Négritude. In the words of Aimé Césaire, 'Blackness is not absence, but refusal.' The fact that the gesture itself was often made from the genial surroundings of a Paris café, that it was often an affair of the intellect and emotions rather than of manners or ways of life, does not alter its cardinal importance in the development of modern African poetry. The gesture of Négritude embraces a good deal of the poetry in this book, notably that of Senghor, David Diop, Birago Diop, and the Congolese poets U Tam'si and Bolamba. Without some understanding of it, at least in its historical importance, it is impossible to see any shape in the poetic events of the continent over the past twenty years.

The two poets of Madagascar included here, though enthusiastically embraced by Senghor in his exciting *Anthologie de la nouvelle poésie nègre et malgache* (1948), do not belong entirely in the company of their French African contemporaries. Madagascar was the last part of the African world (with which it is now generally classed) to fall under French rule, yet it was the first in which France practised her cultural policy of *assimilation* with even limited effectiveness. The island was not fully occupied by French troops until 1896, and one of the first acts of the strongly anti-clerical metropolitan government was to close down hundreds of mission schools which had already sprung up there. Soon, however, this policy was reversed and France began producing a small Malagasy élite which could assist in the administration of the country. By the 1920s Madagascar had produced a poet of genius who wrote and thought in French, Jean-Joseph Rabéarivelo. This tragic and brilliant figure, with his passionate love of French literature, was so effectively *assimilé* that he committed suicide in 1937 when the local officials persistently blocked his efforts to go to France. His poetry is undoubtedly influenced by the symbolists; there are echoes of Laforgue's Pierrotesque tone in *What invisible rat*, and perhaps of Rimbaud in *Cactus*. Yet his poetry is very strongly itself. The brilliant intensity of its imagery, like Leconte de Lisle's, may be the feature which most marks him as a child of the tropics. Rabéarivelo never hectors the reader in the modern didactic manner, but instead leads him confidently into his own visionary world. His ability to sustain, elaborate, and explore a single image throughout an entire poem, as in *Cactus* or *The black glassmaker*, distinguishes him from the more *engagés* poets of French Africa. Furthermore, at the time when Rabéarivelo was writing, Madagascar did not regard itself as part of the African world, a world of which it was only dimly aware.

In Flavien Ranaivo, a more recent poet, Madagascar asserts its own poetic traditions more vigorously. The slangy insolent tone of his verse reveals an authentic inspiration from the popular vernacular songs of the island. *Song of a Young Girl* combines very successfully this lounging gait with a delightful impudence of language, while *Song of a Common Lover* employs the line-by-line ingenuity of the riddling ballad.

Madagascar has a third established poet in Jacques Rabemananjara. He had played a valiant part in his country's liberation, and suffered imprisonment for many years after the savage suppression of the 1947 revolt. He is not represented here because his rhetorical, rather long-winded poetry does not translate well into English and is difficult to quote briefly with proper effect. Much more clearly than the other two, he belongs to the Négritude tradition, and in the company of other poet-politicians like Senghor, Damas, Césaire, and Keita Fodeba.

Senegal is the only part of the African mainland which really witnessed *assimilation* in practice. Elsewhere it was not even attempted until after 1946 and was abandoned altogether as official policy some ten years later. Léopold Sédar Senghor was one of the very few Senegalese to find his way to a French university before the war. Born in 1906 of a Serere family in the little Portuguese settlement of Joal, he came to Paris in 1928 and soon after met the two men with whom he was to be associated as an apostle of Négritude, Aimé Césaire of Martinique and Léon Damas of French Guinea. It was Damas who first found a voice for the group of Negro 'exiles' in Paris in his bitter, staccato volume *Pigments*, issued by G.L.M. in 1937 and later destroyed by the French police:

> . . . my hatred thrived on the margin of culture
> the margin of theories the margin of idle talk
> with which they stuffed me since birth
> even though all in me aspired to be Negro
> while they ransack my Africa.*

But it was Césaire who two years later coined the word *Négritude* and established himself as the chief poet and inspiration of the movement with his great poem *Cahier d'un retour au pays natal*. This poem was soon afterwards hailed by André Breton as a surrealist masterpiece; but in his ambitious survey of neo-African culture, *Muntu* (Faber, 1961), the German scholar Janheinz Jahn has argued that Césaire's purpose was far more rational and deliberate than a mere 'dive into the unconscious'. When he arranges certain words in an apparently surrealist paradox he does so in order to break their conventional association and make them anew. Thus he writes of the imprisoned hero Toussaint L'Ouverture, dying in the Jura mountains amid the snows of the Northern winter:

> What I am
> is a man alone imprisoned in
> white
> is a man alone who defies
> the white cries of white death
> (TOUSSAINT, TOUSSAINT
> L'OUVERTURE)
> is a man who fascin-
> ates the white hawk of white death

* From *Pigments* by L. G. Damas (G.L.M., Paris, 1937), translation by Ulli Beier.

18

is a man alone in the sterile sea of white sand
is an old darky braced against
the waters of the sky*

Against Jahn it could be argued that, although Césaire's ideology embraces Négritude, his technique is unmistakably surrealist, and to describe it as peculiarly Negro is a piece of critical obscurantism. It is true that Senghor, who also began to write at this time, occasionally uses language in a rather similar way; but he does so with a characteristic rhetorical amplitude which woos the reader instead of shocking him.

Perhaps I was the light which slept upon your
    forms fluid as a statue
The green light which gilded you, which made
    you the Sun of my splendid night†

In Senghor's poetry all the familiar themes of Négritude appear one by one; the pervasive presence of the dead and their protective guiding influence upon the living (In *Memoriam, Night of Sine*); the devastation of ancient Africa and its culture by white Europe (*Paris in the Snow*); the harsh rigidity of the modern West and its desperate need for the complementing qualities of Africa (*New York*); the warm triumphant beauty of African woman (*You Held the Black Face*). But a poem like *Luxembourg 1939* shows another facet of Senghor, his profound love and understanding of what is great and enduring in Western achievement, his need to live in both cultures, to be what he himself calls 'a cultural mulatto'.

Many of these themes recur in the slender, exquisite verses of Birago Diop, a contemporary of Senghor's who has spent far more of his life in Africa, working as a government official. But in the angry, stabbing lines of

* From *Cahier d'un retour au pays natal* by Aimé Césaire (Présence Africaine, Paris, 1956), pp. 45–6, translation by Gerald Moore.

† From *D'autres chants* (published in *Éthiopiques*, Éditions du Seuil, Paris, 1956), translation by Gerald Moore.

David Diop, killed in an air crash at the age of thirty-three, there is no room for gentle nostalgia or forgiveness. His poems move inexorably towards a triumphant affirmation. He does not *hope* for better things, he *commands* them by the power of the word, just as Agostinho Neto does from the coffee-fields of Angola.

In the Congolese poets U Tam'si and Bolamba the influence of Césaire is much more direct. Instead of the sonorous monotony of Senghor, they offer a series of intense images related to each other by association rather than by any immediately perceptible string of meaning. This technique is not uniformly successful, though, at their best, they both produce some memorable poems and brilliant images, like U Tam'si's:

> My race remembers
> The taste of bronze drunk hot.

With the poets of English-speaking Africa we move to an entirely different world, one which knows little of Négritude, and generally dislikes what it knows. The dismissive comment of Mphahlele ('To us in the multi-racial communities ... Négritude is just so much intellectual talk, a cult') can be matched by the Nigerian Wole Soyinka, who ridicules the idea of a Tiger having to proclaim his tigritude. This attitude is a trifle unfair, but its origins are not difficult to find. To begin with, the taste for literary 'movements' is much more Gallic than Anglo-Saxon, and there can be little doubt that the intellectual attitudes of the colonial powers have affected their respective former subjects profoundly. Again, Britain never pursued a policy of cultural *assimilation* but, characteristically, had no cultural policy at all. Consequently, there was far less to react *against*, emotionally and intellectually, than in French Africa. But correspondingly, it was considerably longer before a generation of West Africans grew up who felt able to write English with real confidence and fluency. At a time when Senghor and others were already

publishing in Parisian literary reviews, Nigeria and Ghana
had nothing to show but a few verses strongly influenced
by missionary hymns and slogans, reflecting an attitude
which would make any Négritude poet see red:

> My simple fathers
> In childlike faith believed all things;
> It cost them much
> And their offspring lost a lot;
> They questioned not the lies of magic
> And fetish seemed to have some logic.*

So wrote the Nigerian Denis Osadebey only about a dozen
years ago. Similar sentiments are still occasionally to be
found in Nigerian poetry, which shows how thoroughly
the job of *de*similation, at least, was accomplished. Here a
Nigerian student, writing only two or three years ago,
reflects smugly how his ancestors gibbered with super-
stitious terror at the mere sight of a sunrise:

> What in ancestral days was fear
> In me is grandeur;
> What in ages gone was dread,
> In me is splendour†

Other pioneer poets of English-speaking Africa were
Dei-Anang of Ghana and H. Carey Thomas of Liberia.
These writers show rather more respect for indigenous
culture, but their handling of the theme is somewhat super-
ficial. Thus Carey Thomas points the opposite moral from
Osadebey in equally flat language:

> Be warned:
> That palefaced strangers
> With unhallowed feet
> Profane this heritage our fathers gave.‡

Recently poetry of this recognizably 'pioneer' type has

---

* Six lines from Denis Osadebey, quoted by Ulli Beier in *Black
Orpheus*, No. 1.

† Four lines by J. D. Ekwere, quoted from *Nigerian Student Verse*
(Ibadan, 1959).

‡ Four lines from H. Carey Thomas, quoted by Ulli Beier in *Black
Orpheus*, No. 1.

begun to appear in East Africa also. The young Kikuyu poet Joe Mutiga writes of the desecration of holy ground by the plantation of new crops:

> Our customs are dug up,
> And put aside, like the grass
> On which the dancer trod,
> And foreign crops implanted;
> And we pass by, eyes on the ground,
> Submitting to the foreign as ours.*

Poets like these have performed a useful function by re-establishing poetry as an occupation for educated men, and their verses are often of great political and sociological interest; but their failure to penetrate the rich traditions either of English or of vernacular poetry afflicts their work with a total lack of style. An anthology of these poems would be an important and moving document in the history of African nationalism. In this anthology they are not included because they cannot be classified as 'modern', in the sense that they do not represent a fresh exploration of language.

It was not until about five years ago that a new generation of poets began to show themselves, notably in Nigeria. With the exception of Gabriel Okara, all these young poets studied at University College, Ibadan. Hence they were able to acquire a literary culture without suffering the sense of alienation and exile which afflicted the black writers gathered in Paris twenty and thirty years ago. Having grown up and been educated in a purely African environment, their work is extraordinarily free from slogans or stereotypes. They are eclectic in their choice of influences, which range from Dylan Thomas, Pound, and Hopkins to Shakespeare and even Aeschylus; yet out of these, each has compounded a strongly individual voice. Wole Soyinka, for instance, who studied at Ibadan before moving to Britain, is the only African poet to date who

* From *To the Ceremonial Mugumbo* by Joe Mutiga, quoted from *Transition*, 3 (Kampala, 1962).

deploys a gift for light, sophisticated irony (*Telephone Conversation, My Next-door Neighbour*). Okara is an introspective, withdrawn poet, whose best work has great beauty and resonance. Poems like *One Night at Victoria Beach* and *The Snowflakes Sail Gently Down* are among the finest things yet to come out of Nigeria. Frank Aig-Imoukhuede has demonstrated the humorous possibilities of pidgin. Does it, perhaps, also have possibilities for pathos?

Jahn has argued in *Muntu* that the genius of African poetry is collective:

In African poetry . . . the expression is always in the service of the content; it is never a question of expressing *oneself*, but of expressing *something* . . . Nor is the African poet ever concerned with his inner nature, with his individuality.*

Like so many pronouncements on African poetry, this does not seem especially true, except to the extent that it is true of all good poetry – do not all poets speak for mankind? A poem like John Pepper Clark's *Night Rain* tingles in every line with the sense of individual experience in a particular time and place. In general, these young poets do not seem at all intent upon expressing the collective African soul, nor do they clamour in every line about being black and proud of it. The maturity and confidence of their writing is one of its most encouraging aspects.

It is interesting to see the use which has been made of vernacular poetry by two of these English-speaking poets, George Awoonor-Williams of Ghana and Mazisi Kunene of South Africa. Both have understood and assimilated the cryptic, rather oracular quality of much vernacular imagery. This has given both freshness and weight to their language. Both, incidentally, come from areas where a great deal of fine vernacular poetry has been collected, Eweland and Zululand.

Much of the poetry from Portuguese Africa is little

* *Muntu*, p. 148.

more than a cry of sheer agony and loss. These territories are still politically and socially in a condition from which most of Africa emerged many years ago. The tiny group of *assimilados* (about 5,000 in Angola, after over 400 years of coastal occupation) provides the principal target of government repression. Dr Agostinho Neto, for instance, was imprisoned in Portugal for over two years until his recent escape. Yet, if few of these poets can write of anything but their immediate dilemma, their work is testimony enough to the unquenchable spirit of their humanity. An exception is Valente Malangatana who, alone among the poets in this collection, is also a painter of distinction. Like the Haitian painter–poet Max Pinchinat, his imagery has great immediacy and presence, a presence which is more than visual:

> and I all fresh, fresh
> breathed gently, wrapped in my napkins.

His two poems seem to us among the most beautiful and rewarding in the whole volume.

Few writers on African poetry can resist the temptation to pontificate. It is interesting to see to what extent these generalizations can be squared with the reality of modern African writing as represented here. For a starting-point let us take a statement like this, of Senghor's:

Monotony of tone, that is what distinguishes poetry from prose, it is the seal of Négritude, the incantation which opens the way to essential things, the Forces of the Cosmos.*

In point of fact, it is only in Senghor's own work that a monotony of this kind is exhibited, and there it is only tolerable because of the splendour of his musical effects:

> Que j'écoute, dans la case enfumée que visite un
>   reflet d'âmes propices
> Ma tête sur ton sein chaud comme un dang au sortir
>   du feu et fumant

* *Éthiopiques*, p. 120.

Que je respire l'odeur de nos Morts, que je recueille
  et redise leur voix vivante, que j'appreuve à
Vivre avant de descendre, au delà du plongeur, dans
  les hautes profondeurs du sommeil.*

David Diop exhibits a certain monotony of *content*, but his movement is too fierce and swift to permit any monotony of style. Could it be that Senghor was merely vindicating his own sonority?

Again, Jahn takes Jean-Paul Sartre to task for having argued in *L'Orphée noir* that Negro poetry is 'the true revolutionary poetry of our time', and that Négritude is the voice of a particular historical moment, when the black race has given tongue to its revolt against white rule. Against this Jahn argues, somewhat primly, that neo-African poetry is not revolutionary at all, but a return to authentic tradition, and that Négritude, far from being the voice of a particular historical moment, is the style in which all African poetry must henceforth be written:

Once for all it took the stain from Africa; it demonstrated that poetry and literature were not only possible in the African manner and out of an African attitude of mind, but that *only such poetry was legitimate* [editors' italics].†

Yet already it begins to look as though Sartre was right. In the last few years there have been signs that the wellspring of Négritude is running dry. The great period was in the forties and early fifties, and since then Césaire, Damas, and Senghor have all been notably unproductive. Birago Diop has published only one slim volume of verse in twenty years. David Diop was killed after writing only a handful of poems and before it was possible to say in what direction his style might have moved. Meanwhile the centre of poetic activity seems to have shifted from Senegal–Paris to Nigeria, where the last five years have seen a remarkable upsurge. And, as already pointed out, these young poets 'of English expression' are not merely indif-

* From *Nuit de Sine* (French text).
† *Muntu*, p. 207.

ferent to, but actually hostile towards, the concept of Négritude.

The answer may be that Négritude has served its purpose in giving neo-African poets a bridgehead and a point of departure. But as Africa moves into independence, the conflicts at the core of Négritude become more and more apparent. It is no coincidence that the word itself was coined by a West Indian, or that he should also have written the most extended poetic exposition of it. The situation of the black West Indian was always essentially different from that of the continental African, and has become increasingly so as Africa itself has passed back into African hands. The black man in Haiti, Cuba, Puerto Rico, Martinique, or Jamaica grew up in a permanent state of exile. He had no name, no tolerated religion, and scarcely any distinct culture of his own, yet until recently he could not expect any position of power or influence in the new mixed societies which had been built upon his labours. Without even knowing, in the vast majority of cases, from which part of Africa his ancestors came, he was obliged to build up a romantic, idealized vision of 'Guinea', a kind of heaven to which all good Negroes go when they die:

> It's the long road to Guinea
> Death takes you there.*

His dilemma has been perfectly expressed by the Cuban poet Nicolas Guillén, who finds nothing except his colour to distinguish him from those who reject him and who is therefore obliged to investigate the meaning of that colour afresh:

> ... All my skin (I should have said so)
> all my skin – does it really come
> from that Spanish marble statue? And my
>   fearful voice

* From *Guinea* by Jacques Roumain, quoted from *The Poetry of the Negro* (New York, 1949).

the harsh cry from my gorge? And all my bones
do they come from there? . . .
Are you quite sure?
Is there nothing else, only that which you wrote
that which you sealed
with a sign of wrath. . . .
Do you not see these drums in my eyes?
Do you not see these drums hammering out
two dry tears?
Have I not got an ancestor of night
with a large black mark
(blacker than the skin)
a large mark
written with a whip?
Have I got not an ancestor
from Mandingo, the Congo, Dahomey?*

One reaction to this dilemma was to plunge into a glorifica-
tion of sensuality – blood, drums, rhythmic ecstasy – such
as we find in a poem like *Rumba* by José Tallet:

The climax of passion, the dancers are trembling
and ecstasy presses José to the ground.
The Bongo is thundering and in a mad whirl
the daemon has broken Tomasa's limbs.
Piqui-tiqui-pan, piqui-tiqui-pan!
Piqui-tiqui-pan, piqui-tiqui-pan!
The blackish Tomasa now falls to the ground
and down also falls Ché Encarnación.
there they are rolling, convulsing, and twitching,
with whirling drum and raging Bongó
the rumba now fades with con-con-co-mabó!
And pa-ca, pa-ca, pa-ca, pa-ca!
Pam! Pam! Pam!†

It was these attitudes of alienation and protest which gave
rise to the literary movement of Negrismo in Cuba during
the late twenties, and to a similar movement in Haiti at
about the same time. And these same Caribbean movements are the direct ancestors of Négritude.

* Akanji's translation of *The Name* in *Black Orpheus*, No. 7.
† Akanji's translation of *Rumba* in *Black Orpheus*, No. 7.

It is interesting that Senghor's great anthology of 1948, the *chef d'œuvre* of Négritude, should contain the work of only three poets from continental Africa, and those three all from Senegal. For it was in Senegal that a handful of African intellectuals were treated to the full rigours of *assimilation*, and later to those of exile – albeit a voluntary exile in Paris. Naturally, the passionate chords of Césaire found an echo in their hearts. Naturally, too, they found less echo in the hearts of poets brought up and educated in the bosom of a functioning African society which, even at the full tide of colonialism, never truly resembled the Caribbean situation.

This is what makes it so dangerous for critics to try and establish a literary orthodoxy, in the manner of Jahn in *Muntu*:

Whether the work of an author whatever his colour, belongs to Western or African culture, depends on whether we find in it those criteria of African culture which we have set forth in the preceding chapters.*

Thus Jahn establishes himself as the keeper of the narrow gate which leads to the African Parnassus. Fortunately, as the following pages show, African poetry is already too rich and various to follow one path only.

Probably the nearest thing to an acceptable generalization about African poetry has been made by Senghor:

The word here is more than the image, it is the *analogous* image, without even the help of metaphor or comparison. It is enough to name the thing, and the sense appears beneath the sign.†

This process is essentially one of verbal magic: the poet-magus *makes* by naming. It undoubtedly lies at the root of all poetry, but it is probably closer to the surface of the poet's mind in Africa than elsewhere because of the recent arrival of literacy in the area, and because he inhabits a

Muntu, p. 195.
† *Éthiopiques*, p. 108.

society where a vast body of traditional ritual, dance, song, poetry, and story is still alive. In a recent article on Ife, William Fagg and Frank Willett have argued that, because he worked in perishable materials, the African carver was forced continually to renew his communion with the gods, to 'make' them afresh. A parallel attitude is expressed by Senghor, who is happiest when his poetry is sung to music in the traditional style and so passes into the mainstream of tradition. In discussing poetic diction he writes:

A poem is like a passage of jazz, where the execution is just as important as the text. . . . I still think that the poem is not complete until it is sung, words and music together.*

And in *Congo* he expresses contempt for the 'permanence' of ink, as compared with the true permanence of rhythmic recreation:

> Oho! Congo oho! to beat out your great name on the
>   waters on the rivers on all memory
> May I move the voice of the kòras Koyaté. The scribe's
>   ink has no memory.†

In compiling this anthology, we have imposed certain limitations upon ourselves. We have confined ourselves to black writers and to texts originally composed in one or other of the European languages spoken in Africa. The first restriction is a matter of definition – African. A collection of this title might logically include the work of all good poets resident in Africa or of African background, whether black, arab, Indian, or white. This would imply the inclusion of such well-anthologized poets as Roy Campbell, William Plomer, and Guy Butler, as well as the various Africaans writers. It seemed to us that such a collection would lack the more particular significance to be found in an anthology of poetry by black Africans, who at least share the experience of a historic awakening and have not hitherto been assembled for study in a convenient form.

* *Éthiopiques*, pp. 121 and 123.
† From *Congo*, published in *Éthiopiques*.

The second limitation is a matter of feasibility. There is poetry awaiting collection in hundreds of African vernaculars. But how is one to make a critical selection without being fully familiar with all the vernaculars concerned? How much of this poetry could be legitimately regarded as 'modern'? And how, having made a selection, could adequate translations be secured? The present dominance of European languages in African creative writing may be temporary, but there is no denying its existence or the strength of the factors making towards it.

Our concept of the modern is perhaps more difficult to define. In part it is simply a matter of quality; hence the exclusion of the rather tractarian verse of the West African pioneers. In part it is a matter of the poets' awareness of the modern idiom in European and American poetry. It is this awareness that enables them to use their respective languages without distracting archaism and in a way that appeals instantly to the contemporary ear.

The most important limitation we imposed was the attempt to set a high standard and to include only those poems which have other claims to attention than the mere fact of having been written by Africans. The cause of literature has been poorly served already by uncritical selection. We thought it indefensible to include bad poems for the sake of keeping everyone happy. Furthermore, anthologies based on a sense of duty rather than of pleasure are always unreadable.

The result of this policy is that some countries, such as Senegal and Nigeria, are well represented, while others do not appear at all. This is an interesting fact in itself; part of the function of an anthology of this kind is to bring out creative strength where it exists. We believe that the balance of selection here, apparently so weighted towards West Africa, represents the actual situation of African poetry at the moment. An anthology compiled five years hence may be able to announce a new pattern.*

*Such a pattern is, in fact, already apparent in the present edition.

Finally, we should like to thank all those poets who have allowed us to reprint their published works and to look over their unpublished manuscripts. Their generosity has made this anthology possible. Special thanks are also due to Alan Ryder, who translated all the Portuguese texts, except Neto's *Farewell at the Moment of Parting*, translated by the editors, and the two poems by Malangatana translated by Dorothy Guedes and Philippa Rumsey. Thanks are also due to Arnold von Bradshaw for his translation of Senghor's *New York*. All the other translations are the work of the editors. We hope that this collection will convince even the most sceptical that African poetry not only exists, but is among the most original and exciting now being written anywhere in the world.

Preface to second edition

WHEN this anthology first appeared, only five years ago, we suggested that the new African poetry in European languages was entering a period of efflorescence. The fact that it is already necessary to prepare a new and greatly enlarged edition seems to bear this out. It is necessary because an anthology of this kind aims, as far as possible, to keep abreast of what is moving within the art. This immediacy may have its penalties, lacking the detachment of the editor who gazes back over a greater distance of time. Yet it equally has the courage of its convictions, and may succeed in breathing into its pages a little of that original excitement of discovery and selection.

Several of the poets included in the first edition have since published one or more volumes of poetry, and an attempt has been made, so far as space permits, to give some account of their recent development. Some, such as Okigbo, Awoonor-Williams and Neto, have refined and developed a style already present in their early work. Others, like Tchicaya U Tam'si, seem always ready to surprise us with a fresh burst of power or a new direction. U Tam'si has now published five books and his poetry has grown in stature with each one.

Among the new poets there are surprises too. The sombre music of Brutus's *At a Funeral* gives a new dimension to South African poetry. Close by one finds the delightful ironic humour of Yambo and Kayo, or the thoughtful honesty of Dipoko's *Our Life* and Ologoudou's

Liberty. These things alone would make the preparation of a second edition worthwhile.

Once again our thanks go to all those poets who have made their work available to us. Of the poems newly translated from the French, *My Days Overgrown* was done by Ulli Beier and all the rest by Gerald Moore. Neto's *African Poem* and *Kinaxixi* was translated from the Portuguese by W. S. Merwin.

Madagascar

Jean-Joseph Rabéarivelo

Four poems from *Traduits de la nuit*:

2

What invisible rat
come from the walls of night
gnaws at the milky cake of the moon?
Tomorrow morning,
when it has gone,
there will be bleeding marks of teeth.

Tomorrow morning
those who have drunk all night
and those who have abandoned their cards,
blinking at the moon
will stammer out:
'Whose is that sixpence
that rolls over the green table?'
'Ah!' one of them will add,
'our friend has lost everything
and killed himself!'

And all will snigger
and, staggering, will fall.
The moon will no longer be there:
the rat will have carried her into his hole.

3

The hide of the black cow is stretched,
stretched but not set to dry,
stretched in the sevenfold shadow.
But who has killed the black cow,
dead without having lowed, dead without having roared,
dead without having once been chased
over that prairie flowered with stars?

She who calves in the far half of the sky.

Stretched is the hide
on the sounding-box of the wind
that is sculptured by the spirits of sleep.

And the drum is ready
when the new-born calf,
her horns crowned with spear grass
leaps
and grazes the grass of the hills.

It reverberates there
and its incantations will become dreams
until the moment when the black cow lives again,
white and pink
before a river of light.

4

She
whose eyes are prisms of sleep
and whose lids are heavy with dreams,
she whose feet are planted in the sea
and whose shiny hands appear
full of corals and blocks of shining salt.

She will put them in little heaps beside a misty gulf
and sell them to naked sailors

whose tongues have been cut out,
until the rain begins to fall.

Then she will disappear
and we shall only see
her hair spread by the wind
like a bunch of seaweed unravelling,
and perhaps some tasteless grains of salt.

17

The black glassmaker
whose countless eyeballs none has ever seen,
whose shoulders none has overlooked,
that slave all clothed in pearls of glass,
who is strong as Atlas
and who carries the seven skies on his head,
one would think that the vast river of clouds might carry
    him away,
the river in which his loincloth is already wet.

A thousand particles of glass
fall from his hands
but rebound towards his brow
shattered by the mountains
where the winds are born.

And you are witness of his daily suffering
and of his endless task;
you watch his thunder-riddled agony
until the battlements of the East re-echo
the conches of the sea –
but you pity him no more
and do not even remember that his sufferings begin again
each time the sun capsizes.

Cactus

(from Presque-songes)

That multitude of moulded hands
holding out flowers to the azure sky
that multitude of fingerless hands
unshaken by the wind
they say that a hidden source
wells from their untainted palms
they say that this inner source
refreshes thousands of cattle
and numberless tribes, wandering tribes
in the frontiers of the South.

Fingerless hands, springing from a source,
Moulded hands, crowning the sky.

Here, when the flanks of the City were still as green
as moonbeams glancing from the forests,
when they still left bare the hills of Iarive
crouching like bulls upthrust,
it was upon rocks too steep even for goats
that they hid, to protect their sources,
these lepers sprouting flowers.

Enter the cave from which they came
if you seek the origin of the sickness which ravages them –
origin more shrouded than the evening
and further than the dawn –
but you will know no more than I.
The blood of the earth, the sweat of the stone,
and the sperm of the wind,
which flow together in these palms
have melted their fingers
and replaced them with golden flowers.

Flavien Ranaivo

Song of a Young Girl

Oaf
the young man who lives down there
beside the threshing floor for rice;
like two banana-roots
on either side the village ditch,
we gaze on each other,
we are lovers,
but he won't marry me.
Jealous
his mistress I saw two days since at the wash house
coming down the path against the wind.
She was proud;
was it because she wore a lamba thick
and studded with coral
or because they are newly bedded?
However it isn't the storm
that will flatten the delicate reed,
nor the great sudden shower
at the passage of a cloud
that will startle out of his wits
the blue bull.
I am amazed;
the big sterile rock
survived the rain of the flood
and it's the fire that crackles
the bad grains of maize.

Such this famous smoker
who took tobacco
when there was no more hemp to burn.
A foot of hemp?
– Sprung in Andringitra,
spent in Ankaratra,
no more than cinders to us.
False flattery
stimulates love a little
but the blade has two edges;
why change what is natural?
– If I have made you sad
look at yourself in the water of repentance,
you will decipher there a word I have left.
Good-bye, whirling puzzle,
I give you my blessing:
wrestle with the crocodile,
here are your victuals and three water-lily flowers
for the way is long.

Song of a Common Lover

Don't love me, my sweet,
like your shadow
for shadows fade at evening
and I want to keep you
right up to cockcrow;
nor like pepper
which makes the belly hot
for then I couldn't take you
when I'm hungry;
nor like a pillow
for we'd be together in the hours of sleep
but scarcely meet by day;

nor like rice
for once swallowed you think no more of it;
nor like soft speeches
for they quickly vanish;
nor like honey,
sweet indeed but too common.
Love me like a beautiful dream,
your life in the night,
my hope in the day;
like a piece of money,
ever with me on earth,
and for the great journey
a faithful comrade;
like a calabash,
intact, for drawing water;
in pieces, bridges for my guitar.

Senegal

Léopold Sédar Senghor

In Memoriam

It is Sunday.

I fear the crowd of my brothers with stony faces.

From my tower of glass filled with pain, the nagging Ancestors

I gaze at roofs and hills in the fog

In the silence – the chimneys are grave and bare.

At their feet sleep my dead, all my dreams are dust

All my dreams, the liberal blood spills all along the streets, mixing with the blood of the butcheries.

And now, from this observatory as from a suburb

I watch my dreams float vaguely through the streets, lie at the hills' feet

Like the guides of my race on the banks of Gambia or Saloum,

Now of the Seine, at the feet of these hills.

Let me think of my dead!

Yesterday it was Toussaint, the solemn anniversary of the sun

And no remembrance in any cemetery.

Ah, dead ones who have always refused to die, who have known how to fight death

By Seine or Sine, and in my fragile veins pushed the invincible blood,

Protect my dreams as you have made your sons, wanderers on delicate feet.

Oh Dead, protect the roofs of Paris in the Sunday fog

The roofs which guard my dead
That from the perilous safety of my tower I may descend
   to the streets
To join my brothers with blue eyes
With hard hands.

Night of Sine

Woman, rest on my brow your balsam hands, your hands
   gentler than fur.
The tall palmtrees swinging in the nightwind
Hardly rustle. Not even cradlesongs,
The rhythmic silence rocks us.
Listen to its song, listen to the beating of our dark blood,
   listen
To the beating of the dark pulse of Africa in the mist of
   lost villages.
Now the tired moon sinks towards its bed of slack
   water,
Now the peals of laughter even fall asleep, and the bards
   themselves
Dandle their heads like children on the backs of their
   mothers.
Now the feet of the dancers grow heavy and heavy grows
   the tongue of the singers.
This is the hour of the stars and of the night that dreams
And reclines on this hill of clouds, draped in her long
   gown of milk.
The roofs of the houses gleam gently. What are they telling
   so confidently to the stars?
Inside the hearth is extinguished in the intimacy of bitter
   and sweet scents.
Woman, light the lamp of clear oil, and let the children in
   bed talk about their ancestors, like their parents.

Listen to the voice of the ancients of Elissa. Like we, exiled,

They did not want to die, lest their seminal flood be lost in the sand.

Let me listen in the smoky hut for the shadowy visit of propitious souls,

My head on your breast glowing, like a kuskus ball smoking out of the fire,

Let me breathe the smell of our dead, let me contemplate and repeat their living voice, let me learn

To live before I sink, deeper than the diver, into the lofty depth of sleep.

Luxembourg 1939

This morning at the Luxembourg, this autumn at the Luxembourg, as I lived and relived my youth

No loafers, no water, no boats upon the water, no children, no flowers.

Ah! the September flowers and the sunburnt cries of children who defied the coming winter.

Only two old boys trying to play tennis.

This autumn morning without children – the children's theatre is shut!

This Luxembourg where I cannot trace my youth, those years fresh as the lawns.

My dreams defeated, my comrades despairing, can it be so?

Behold them falling like leaves with the leaves, withered and wounded trampled to death the colour of blood

To be shovelled into what common grave?

I do not know this Luxembourg, these soldiers mounting guard.

They have put guns to protect the whispering retreat of
    Senators,
They have cut trenches under the bench where I first learnt
    the soft flowering of lips.
That notice again! Ah yes, dangerous youth!
I watch the leaves fall into the shelters, into the ditches,
    into the trenches
Where the blood of a generation flows
Europe is burying the yeast of nations and the hope of
    newer races.

Totem

I must hide him in my innermost veins
The Ancestor whose stormy hide is shot with lightning and
    thunder
My animal protector, I must hide him
That I may not break the barriers of scandal:
He is my faithful blood that demands fidelity
Protecting my naked pride against
Myself and the scorn of luckier races.

Paris in the Snow

Lord, you visited Paris on the day of your birth
Because it had become paltry and bad.
You purified it with incorruptible cold,
The white death.
This morning even the factory funnels hoisted in harmony
The white flags.
'Peace to all men of good will.'

Lord, you have offered the divided world, divided Europe,
The snow of peace.
And the rebels fired their fourteen hundred cannons
Against the mountains of your peace.
Lord, I have accepted your white cold that burns worse
than salt.
And now my heat melts like snow in the sun.
And I forget
The white hands that loaded the guns that destroyed the
kingdoms,
The hands that whipped the slaves and that whipped you
The dusty hands that slapped you, the white powdered
hands that slapped me
The sure hands that pushed me into solitude and hatred
The white hands that felled the high forest that dominated
Africa,
That felled the Sara, erect and firm in the heart of Africa,
beautiful like the first men that were created by your
brown hands.
They felled the virgin forest to turn into railway sleepers.
They felled Africa's forest in order to save civilization that
was lacking in men.
Lord, I can still not abandon this last hate, I know it, the
hatred of diplomats who show their long teeth
And who will barter with black flesh tomorrow.
My heart, oh lord, has melted like the snow on the roofs of
Paris
In the sun of your Goodness,
It is kind to my enemies, my brothers with the snowless
white hands,
Also because of the hands of dew that lie on my burning
cheeks at night.

Blues

The spring has swept the ice from all my frozen rivers
My young sap trembles at the first caresses along the
tender bark.
But see how in the midst of July I am blinder than the
Arctic winter!
My wings beat and break against the barriers of heaven
No ray pierces the deaf vault of my bitterness.
What sign is there to find? What key to strike?
And how can god be reached by hurling javelins?
Royal Summer of the distant South, you will come too
late, in a hateful September!
In what book can I find the thrill of your reverberation?
And on the pages of what book, on what impossible lips
taste your delirious love?

The impatient fit leaves me. Oh! the dull beat of the rain
on the leaves!
Just play me your 'Solitude', Duke, till I cry myself to
sleep.

The Dead

They are lying out there beside the captured roads, all
along the roads of disaster
Elegant poplars, statues of sombre gods draped in their
long cloaks of gold,
Senegalese prisoners darkly stretched on the soil of France.
In vain they have cut off your laughter, in vain the darker
flower of your flesh,
You are the flower in its first beauty amid a naked absence
of flowers
Black flower with its grave smile, diamond of immemorial
ages.

You are the slime and plasma of the green spring of the world
Of the first couple you are the flesh, the ripe belly the milkiness
You are the sacred increase of the bright gardens of paradise
And the invincible forest, victorious over fire and thunderbolt.
The great song of your blood will vanquish machines and cannons
Your throbbing speech evasions and lies.
No hate in your soul void of hatred, no cunning in your soul void of cunning.
O Black Martyrs immortal race, let me speak the words of pardon.

Prayer to Masks

Black mask, red mask, you black and white masks,
Rectangular masks through whom the spirit breathes,
I greet you in silence!
And you too, my pantherheaded ancestor.
You guard this place, that is closed to any feminine laughter, to any mortal smile.
You purify the air of eternity, here where I breathe the air of my fathers.
Masks of maskless faces, free from dimples and wrinkles,
You have composed this image, this my face that bends over the altar of white paper.
In the name of your image, listen to me!
Now while the Africa of despotism is dying – it is the agony of a pitiable princess
Just like Europe to whom she is connected through the navel,

53

Now turn your immobile eyes towards your children who
  have been called
And who sacrifice their lives like the poor man his last
  garment
So that hereafter we may cry 'here' at the rebirth of the
  world being the leaven that the white flour needs.
For who else would teach rhythm to the world that has
  died of machines and cannons?
For who else should ejaculate the cry of joy, that arouses
  the dead and the wise in a new dawn?
Say, who else could return the memory of life to men with
  a torn hope?
They call us cotton heads, and coffee men, and oily men,
They call us men of death.
But we are the men of the dance whose feet only gain
  power when they beat the hard soil.

Visit

I dream in the intimate semi-darkness of an afternoon.
I am visited by the fatigues of the day,
The deceased of the year, the souvenirs of the decade,
Like the procession of the dead in the village on the horizon
  of the shallow sea.
It is the same sun bedewed with illusions,
The same sky unnerved by hidden presences,
The same sky feared by those who have a reckoning with
  the dead.
And suddenly my dead draw near to me. . . .

All Day Long

All day long, over the long straight rails
Like an inflexible will over the endless sands
Across parched Cayor and Baol where the baobabs twist
 their arms in torment
All day long, all along the line
Past the same little stations, past black girls jostling like
 birds at the gates of schools
All day long, sorely rattled by the iron train and dusty and
 hoarse
Behold me seeking to forget Europe in the pastoral heart
 of Sine!

In what Tempestuous Night

What dark tempestuous night has been hiding your face?
And what claps of thunder frighten you from the bed
When the fragile walls of my breast tremble?
I shudder with cold, trapped in the dew of the clearing.
O, I am lost in the treacherous paths of the forest.
Are these creepers or snakes that entangle my feet?
I slip into the mudhole of fear and my cry is suffocated in a
 watery rattle.
But when shall I hear your voice again, happy luminous
 morn?
When shall I recognize myself again in the laughing mirror
 of eyes, that are large like windows?
And what sacrifice will pacify the white mask of the god-
 dess?
Perhaps the blood of chickens or goats, or the worthless
 blood in my veins?
Or the prelude of my song, the ablution of my pride?

Give me propitious words.

New York
(for jazz orchestra: trumpet solo)

I

New York! At first I was confused by your beauty, by
  those great golden long-legged girls.
So shy at first before your blue metallic eyes, your frosted
  smile
So shy. And the anguish in the depths of skyscraper streets
Lifting eyes hawkhooded to the sun's eclipse.
Sulphurous your light and livid the towers with heads that
  thunderbolt the sky
The skyscrapers which defy the storms with muscles of
  steel and stone-glazed hide.
But two weeks on the bare sidewalks of Manhattan
– At the end of the third week the fever seizes you with the
  pounce of a leopard
Two weeks without rivers or fields, all the birds of the air
Falling sudden and dead on the high ashes of flat rooftops.
No smile of a child blooms, his hand refreshed in my hand,
No mother's breast, but only nylon legs. Legs and breasts
  that have no sweat nor smell.
No tender word for there are no lips, only artificial hearts
  paid for in hard cash
And no book where wisdom may be read. The painter's
  palette blossoms with crystals of coral.
Nights of insomnia oh nights of Manhattan! So agitated
  by flickering lights, while motor-horns howl of empty
  hours
And while dark waters carry away hygienic loves, like
  rivers flooded with the corpses of children.

2

Now is the time of signs and reckonings
New York! Now is the time of manna and hyssop.
You must but listen to the trombones of God, let your
    heart beat in the rhythm of blood, your blood.
I saw in Harlem humming with noise with stately colours
    and flamboyant smells
– It was teatime at the house of the seller of pharmaceutical
    products –
I saw them preparing the festival of night for escape from
    the day.
I proclaim night more truthful than the day.
It was the pure hour when in the streets God makes the
    life that goes back beyond memory spring up
All the amphibious elements shining like suns.
Harlem Harlem! Now I saw Harlem! A green breeze of
    corn springs up from the pavements ploughed by the
    naked feet of dancers
Bottoms waves of silk and sword-blade breasts, water-lily
    ballets and fabulous masks.
At the feet of police-horses roll the mangoes of love from
    low houses.
And I saw along the sidewalks streams of white rum
    streams of black milk in the blue fog of cigars.
I saw the sky in the evening snow cotton-flowers and
    seraphims' wings and sorcerers' plumes.
Listen New York! Oh listen to your male voice of brass
    vibrating with oboes, the anguish choked with tears
    falling in great clots of blood
Listen to the distant beating of your nocturnal heart,
    rhythm and blood of the tom-tom, tom-tom blood and
    tom-tom.

3

New York! I say to you: New York let black blood flow
   into your blood
That it may rub the rust from your steel joints, like an oil
   of life,
That it may give to your bridges the bend of buttocks and
   the suppleness of creepers.
Now return the most ancient times, the unity recovered,
   the reconciliation of the Lion the Bull and the Tree
Thought linked to act, ear to heart, sign to sense.
There are your rivers murmuring with scented crocodiles
   and mirage-eyed manatees. And no need to invent the
   Sirens.
But it is enough to open the eyes to the rainbow of April
And the ears, above all the ears, to God who out of the
   laugh of a saxophone created the heaven and the earth in
   six days.
And the seventh day he slept the great sleep of the Negro.

You Held the Black Face
(for Khalam)

You held the black face of the warrior between your
   hands
Which seemed with fateful twilight luminous.
From the hill I watched the sunset in the bays of your
   eyes.
When shall I see my land again, the pure horizon of your
   face?
When shall I sit at the table of your dark breasts?
The nest of sweet decisions lies in the shade.
I shall see different skies and different eyes,
And shall drink from the sources of other lips, fresher than
   lemons,

I shall sleep under the roofs of other hair, protected from
   storms.
But every year, when the rum of spring kindles the veins
   afresh,
I shall mourn anew my home, and the rain of your eyes
   over the thirsty savannah.

I will Pronounce your Name
(for Tama)

I will pronounce your name, Naëtt, I will declaim you,
   Naëtt!
Naëtt, your name is mild like cinnamon, it is the fragrance
   in which the lemon grove sleeps,
Naëtt, your name is the sugared clarity of blooming coffee
   trees
And it resembles the savannah, that blossoms forth under
   the masculine ardour of the midday sun.
Name of dew, fresher than shadows of tamarind,
Fresher even than the short dusk, when the heat of the day
   is silenced.
Naëtt, that is the dry tornado, the hard clap of lightning
Naëtt, coin of gold, shining coal, you my night, my sun!..
I am your hero, and now I have become your sorcerer, in
   order to pronounce your names.
Princess of Elissa, banished from Futa on the fateful day.

Be not Amazed

Be not amazed beloved, if sometimes my song grows dark,
If I exchange the lyrical reed for the Khalam or the tama
And the green scent of the ricefields, for the swiftly gallop-
   ing war drums.

59

I hear the threats of ancient deities, the furious cannonade
of the god.

Oh, tomorrow perhaps, the purple voice of your bard will
be silent for ever.

That is why my rhythm becomes so fast, that the fingers
bleed on the Khalam.

Perhaps, beloved, I shall fall tomorrow, on a restless earth

Lamenting your sinking eyes, and the dark tom-tom of the
mortars below.

And you will weep in the twilight for the glowing voice
that sang your black beauty.

David Diop

Listen Comrades

Listen comrades of the struggling centuries
To the keen clamour of the Negro from Africa to the
    Americas
They have killed Mamba
As they killed the seven of Martinsville
Or the Madagascan down there in the pale light on the
    prisons
He held in his look comrades
The warm faith of a heart without anguish
And his smile despite agony
Despite the wounds of his broken body
Kept the bright colours of a bouquet of hope
It is true that they have killed Mamba with his white hairs
Who ten times poured forth for us milk and light
I feel his mouth on my dreams
And the peaceful tremor of his breast
And I am lost again
Like a plant torn from the maternal bosom
But no
For there rings out higher than my sorrows
Purer than the morning where the wild beast wakes
The cry of a hundred people smashing their cells
And my blood long held in exile
The blood they hoped to snare in a circle of words
Rediscovers the fervour that scatters the mists
Listen comrades of the struggling centuries

To the keen clamour of the Negro from Africa to the
  Americas
It is the sign of the dawn
The sign of brotherhood which comes to nourish the
  dreams of men.

Your Presence

In your presence I rediscovered my name
My name that was hidden under the pain of separation
I rediscovered the eyes no longer veiled with fever
And your laughter like a flame piercing the shadows
Has revealed Africa to me beyond the snows of yesterday
Ten years my love
With days of illusions and shattered ideas
And sleep made restless with alcohol
The suffering that burdens today with the taste of to-
  morrow
And that turns love into a boundless river
In your presence I have rediscovered the memory of my
  blood
And necklaces of laughter hung around our days
Days sparkling with ever new joys.

The Renegade

My brother you flash your teeth in response to every
  hypocrisy
My brother with gold-rimmed glasses
You give your master a blue-eyed faithful look
My poor brother in immaculate evening dress

Screaming and whispering and pleading in the parlours of
   condescension
We pity you
Your country's burning sun is nothing but a shadow
On your serene 'civilized' brow
And the thought of your grandmother's hut
Brings blushes to your face that is bleached
By years of humiliation and bad conscience
And while you trample on the bitter red soil of Africa
Let these words of anguish keep time with your
   restless step –
Oh I am lonely so lonely here.

Africa

Africa my Africa
Africa of proud warriors in ancestral savannahs
Africa of whom my grandmother sings
On the banks of the distant river
I have never known you
But your blood flows in my veins
Your beautiful black blood that irrigates the fields
The blood of your sweat
The sweat of your work
The work of your slavery
The slavery of your children
Africa tell me Africa
Is this you this back that is bent
This back that breaks under the weight of humiliation
This back trembling with red scars
And saying yes to the whip under the midday sun
But a grave voice answers me
Impetuous son that tree young and strong
That tree there

In splendid loneliness amidst white and faded flowers
That is Africa your Africa
That grows again patiently obstinately
And its fruit gradually acquire
The bitter taste of liberty.

The Vultures

In those days
When civilization kicked us in the face
When holy water slapped our cringing brows
The vultures built in the shadow of their talons
The bloodstained monument of tutelage
In those days
There was painful laughter on the metallic hell of the
    roads
And the monotonous rhythm of the paternoster
Drowned the howling on the plantations
O the bitter memories of extorted kisses
Of promises broken at the point of a gun
Of foreigners who did not seem human
Who knew all the books but did not know love
But we whose hands fertilize the womb of the earth
In spite of your songs of pride
In spite of the desolate villages of torn Africa
Hope was preserved in us as in a fortress
And from the mines of Swaziland to the factories of
    Europe
Spring will be reborn under our bright steps.

To a Black Dancer

Negress my warm rumour of Africa
My land of mystery and my fruit of reason
You are the dance by the naked joy of your smile
By the offering of your breasts and secret powers
You are the dance by the golden tales of marriage nights
By new tempos and more secular rhythms
Negress repeated triumph of dreams and stars
Passive mistress to the koras' assault
You are the dance of giddyness
By the magic of loins restarting the world
You are the dance
And the myths burn around me
Around me the wigs of learning
In great fires of joy in the heaven of your steps
You are the dance
And burn false gods in your vertical flame
You are the face of the initiate
Sacrificing his childhood before the tree-god
You are the idea of All and the voice of the Ancient
Gravely rocketed against our fears
You are the Word which explodes
In showers of light upon the shores of oblivion.

Nigger Tramp

You who move like a battered old dream
A dream transpierced by the blades of the mistral
By what bitter ways
By what muddy wanderings of accepted suffering
By what caravels drawing from isle to isle
The curtains of Negro blood torn from Guinea
Have you carried your old coat of thorns
To the foreign cemetery where you read the sky

I see in your eyes the drooping halts of despair
And dawn restarting the cottonfields and mines
I see Soundiata the forgotten
And Chaka the invincible
Fled to the seabed with the tales of silk and fire
I see all that
Martial music sounding the call to murder
And bellies that burst open amid snowy landscapes
To comfort the fear crouched in the entrails of cities
O my old Negro harvester of unknown lands
Lands of spice where everyone could live
What have they done with the dawn that lifted on your
    brow
With your bright stones and sabres of gold
Now you stand naked in your filthy prison
A quenched volcano exposed to others' laughter
To others' riches
To others' hideous greed
They called you Half-White it was so picturesque
And they shook their great jaws to the roots
Delighted at a joke not malicious in the least
But I what was I doing on your morning of wind and tears
On that morning drowned in spray
Where the ancient crowns perished
What did I do but endure seated upon my clouds
The nightly agonies
The unhealing wounds
The petrified bundles of rags in the camps of disaster
The sand was all blood
And I saw the day like any other day
And I sang Yéba
Yéba like a delirious beast
O buried promise
O forsaken seed
Forgive me Negro guide
Forgive my narrow heart
The belated victories the abandoned armour

Have patience the Carnival is over
I sharpen the hurricane for the furrows of the future
For you we will remake Ghana and Timbuktu
And the guitars shuddering with a thousand strokes
Great mortars booming under the blows
Pestles
Pounding
From house to house
In the coming day.

Birago Diop

Diptych

The Sun hung by a thread
In the depths of the Calabash dyed indigo
Boils the great Pot of Day.
Fearful of the approach of the Daughters of fire
The Shadow squats at the feet of the faithful.
The savannah is bright and harsh
All is sharp, forms and colours.
But in the anguished Silences made by Rumours
Of tiny sounds, neither hollow nor shrill,
Rises a ponderous Mystery,
A Mystery muffled and formless
Which surrounds and terrifies us.

The dark Loincloth pierced with nails of fire
Spread out on the Earth covers the bed of Night.
Fearful at the approach of the Daughters of shadow
The dog howls, the horse neighs
The Man crouches deep in his house.
The savannah is dark,
All is black, forms and colours
And in the anguished Silences made by Rumours
Of tiny sounds infinite or hollow or sharp
The tangled Paths of the Mystery
Slowly reveal themselves
For those who set out
And for those who return.

Omen

A naked sun – a yellow sun
A sun all naked at early dawn
Pours waves of gold over the bank
Of the river of yellow.

A naked sun – a white sun
A sun all naked and white
Pours waves of silver
Over the river of white.

A naked sun – a red sun
A sun all naked and red
Pours waves of red blood
Over the river of red.

Vanity

If we tell, gently, gently
All that we shall one day have to tell,
Who then will hear our voices without laughter,
Sad complaining voices of beggars
Who indeed will hear them without laughter?

If we cry roughly of our torments
Ever increasing from the start of things,
What eyes will watch our large mouths
Shaped by the laughter of big children
What eyes will watch our large mouths?

What heart will listen to our clamouring?
What ear to our pitiful anger
Which grows in us like a tumour
In the black depth of our plaintive throats?

When our Dead come with their Dead
When they have spoken to us with their clumsy voices;
Just as our ears were deaf

To their cries, to their wild appeals
Just as our ears were deaf
They have left on the earth their cries,
In the air, on the water, where they have traced their signs
For us, blind deaf and unworthy Sons
Who see nothing of what they have made
In the air, on the water, where they have traced their signs.

And since we did not understand our dead
Since we have never listened to their cries
If we weep, gently, gently
If we cry roughly of our torments
What heart will listen to our clamouring,
What ear to our sobbing hearts?

Ball

A scroll of blue, an exquisite thought
Moves upwards in a secret accord
And the gentle pink explosion the shade filters
Drowns a woman's perfume in a heavy regret.

The languorous lament of the saxophone
Counts a string of troubles and vague promises
And, jagged or monotonous, its raucous cry
Sometimes awakes a desire I had thought dead.

Stop jazz, you scan the sobs and tears
That jealous hearts keep only to themselves.
Stop your scrap-iron din. Your uproar
Seems like a huge complaint where consent is born.

Viaticum

In one of the three pots
the three pots to which on certain evenings
the happy souls return
the serene breath of the ancestors,
the ancestors who were men,
the forefathers who were wise,
Mother wetted three fingers,
three fingers of her left hand:
the thumb, the index and the next;
I too wetted three fingers,
three fingers of my right hand:
the thumb, the index and the next.

With her three fingers red with blood,
with dog's blood,
with bull's blood,
with goat's blood,
Mother touched me three times.
She touched my forehead with her thumb,
With her index my left breast
And my navel with her middle finger.
I too held my fingers red with blood,
with dog's blood,
with bull's blood,
with goat's blood.
I held my three fingers to the winds
to the winds of the North, to the winds of the Levant,
to the winds of the South, to the winds of the setting sun;
and I raised my three fingers towards the Moon,
towards the full Moon, the Moon full and naked
when she rested deep in the largest pot.
Afterwards I plunged my three fingers in the sand
in the sand that had grown cold.
Then Mother said, 'Go into the world, go!
They will follow your steps in life.'

Since then I go
I follow the pathways
the pathways and roads
beyond the sea and even farther,
beyond the sea and beyond the beyond;
And whenever I approach the wicked,
the Men with black hearts,
whenever I approach the envious,
the Men with black hearts
before me moves the Breath of the Ancestors.

Mali

Ouologuem Yambo

When Negro Teeth Speak

Everyone thinks me a cannibal
But you know how people talk

Everyone sees my red gums but who
Has white ones
Up with tomatoes

Everyone says fewer tourists will come
Now
But you know
We aren't in America and anyway everyone
Is broke

Everyone says it's my fault and is afraid
But look
My teeth are white not red
I haven't eaten anyone

People are wicked and say I gobble
the tourists roasted
Or perhaps grilled
Roasted or grilled I asked them
They fell silent and looked fearfully at my gums
Up with tomatoes

Everyone knows an arable country has agriculture
Up with vegetables

Everyone maintains that vegetables
Don't nourish the grower well

And that I am well-grown for an undeveloped man
Miserable vermin living on tourists
Down with my teeth

Everyone suddenly surrounded me
Fettered
Thrown down prostrated
At the feet of justice

Cannibal or not cannibal
Speak up
Ah you think yourself clever
And try to look proud

Now we'll see you get what's coming to you
What is your last word
Poor condemned man

I shouted up with tomatoes

The men were cruel and the women curious you see
There was one in the peering circle
Who with her voice rattling like the lid of a casserole
Screamed
Yelped
Open him up
I'm sure papa is still inside

The knives being blunt
Which is understandable among vegetarians
Like the Westerners
They grabbed a Gillette blade
And patiently
Crisss
Crasss
Floccc
They opened my belly

A plantation of tomatoes was growing there
Irrigated by streams of palm wine
Up with tomatoes

Gambia

Lenrie Peters

Homecoming

The present reigned supreme
  Like the shallow floods over the gutters
Over the raw paths where we had been,
  The house with the shutters.

Too strange the sudden change
  Of the times we buried when we left
The times before we had properly arranged
  The memories that we kept.

Our sapless roots have fed
  The wind-swept seedlings of another age.
Luxuriant weeds have grown where we led
  The Virgins to the water's edge.

There at the edge of the town
  Just by the burial ground
Stands the house without a shadow
  Lived in by new skeletons.

That is all that is left
  To greet us on the home-coming
After we have paced the world
  And longed for returning.

Song

Clawed green-eyed
Feline of night
Palsy-breasted
Selling old boot
On wet pavement
In hour-glass baskets
Coconut bellied
Unyielding copra
Gland exhausted
Love fatigued
Worm-tunnelled sod
Prostituted fruit of Eve
Edging the Park trees
Like dancing Caterpillars
In folded leaves
Softened by Social Conscience
Hounded by Prudes
Friend of the falling star
Victim of the lonely bed.

We have Come Home

We have come home
From the bloodless war
With sunken hearts
Our boots full of pride –
From the true massacre of the soul
When we have asked
'What does it cost
To be loved and left alone?'

We have come home,
Bringing the pledge
Which is written in rainbow colours

Across the sky – for burial
But it is not the time
To lay wreaths
For yesterday's crimes
Night threatens
Time dissolves
And there is no acquaintance
With tomorrow
The gurgling drums
Echo the star
The forest howls –
And between the trees
The dark sun appears.

We have come home
When the dawn falters
Singing songs of other lands
The Death March
Violating our ears
Knowing all our lore and tears
Determined by the spinning coin.

We have come home
To the green foothills
To drink from the cry
Of warm and mellow birdsong.
To the hot beaches
Where boats go out to sea
Threshing the ocean's harvest
And the harassing, plunging
gliding gulls shower kisses on the waves.
We have come home

Where through the lightning flash
And thundering rain
The Pestilence, the drought
The sodden spirit
Lingers on the sandy road

Supporting the tortured remnants
Of the flesh
That spirit which asks no favour
But to have dignity.

One Long Jump

One long jump
From the early days
When the face was like a globe
Round, revolving, limitless
Sharp incisive like a probe
And eyes which could see
With the completeness of a globe – geometrically
A soft film of brown hairs
And a language of birds and flowers.

One long jump
From the early days
When wave upon wave
Of passion merged
Cutting their losses
Preserving their 'gains'
And beauty tingled the flesh
Like a snake
On the surface of the lake
Yielding her store of comfort
Without deceit
Without fictitious powers of support
And no didactic analyses
To know that milk was sweet.

One long jump
And never another
Never quite the same
Because things get mouldy

In the grave
and milk loses its taste
On the coated tongue
Bartered birthrite
Like the chaste membrane
Is lost for good
So we can never arrive
At the beginning
To couch in the blue light
Of the primaeval hive
Except in the dissolution of the flesh
And early strength never returns
To oppose the grinding artificialities
Or to marvel at the rose

One long jump
The first and last
And no progression
So take it well.
Looking back upsets
The balanced wheel
Too tired if we arrive
It is enough
To seek the short cut
To the grave.

Parachute Men

Parachute Men say
The first jump
Takes the breath away
Feet in the air disturbs
Till you get used to it.

Solid ground
Is not where you left it

As you plunge down
Perhaps head first
As you listen to
Your arteries talking
You learn to sustain hope

Suddenly you are only
Holding an open umbrella
In a windy place
As the warm earth
Reaches out to you
Reassures you
The vibrating interim is over

You try to land
Where the green grass yields
And carry your pack
Across the fields.

The violent arrival
Puts out the joint
Earth has nowhere to go
You are at the starting point

Jumping across worlds
In condensed time
After the awkward fall
We are always at the starting point.

She Came in Silken Drapes

She came in silken drapes
And naked breasts;
'Veiled' Artemis; seated
On an eagle's nest
Brandishing the sword

And that forbidden thing
Less clumsy in a dream

She handed me the word
Sealed in cotton-wool
Tied in an endless riddle –
Love and loveless hate
Poison of the Coral Snake
Infinitely tender to see
Like Saturn's Mystery.

Gentle winged Butterfly
With the voiceless cry, by day –
Huntress of crippled manhood
Unequal tyrant, by night –
Visiting the caves of Hysterus
Where the wounded leopard sleeps
In the green light of peace.

Walking in the mist
Among the chambered Monuments
Crowded like icicles
In the patient current
Which feeds by exhaustion,
She smooths her wrinkles
And prepares for the assault.

Love, lustreless word
A thousand times misused
As often bathed in blood.
Let me wash you
Like the frenzied gold sifter

Let me lead you
Through the dense crowd,
And over the phallic mound
To the crystal spring
Where I have found
The purest living thing.

Ivory Coast

Charles Nokan

My Head is Immense

My head is immense
I have a toad's eyes
A horn stands on the nape of my neck
But a magical music surges
from me.
What tree exhales such rare
perfume?
Dark beauty, how can you spring
from a toad's wallow? How can you
flow from lonely ugliness?
You who look on, you think
that the voice of my instrument
buys my freedom, that I am fluidity, thought
which flies.
No, there is nothing in me
but a pool of sadness.

Joseph Miezan Bognini

My Days Overgrown

My days overgrown with coffee blossoms,
My childhood has lost its meaning.

The hatred one has eaten
Can never be destroyed.

Misfortune, I am misfortune,
And my shadow has betrayed me;
Suffering, I am suffering,
Inexperienced at the breast of mankind.

I wish you were music
Rocking the thirsty hearts from afar.

You will carry me away one day
Wrapped in white robes
Into another world.

I have become a grain of sand
Drifting along trembling beaches.

You will bring me asylum
That knows the pain of this night.

You changed your face,
I took you by the hand

And we spent happy days.

Earth and Sky

Earth and sky are infinities
Where our cries cannot venture

I have fixed my head between two stones
Seeking the Shelterer in vain.

Only your splendour sets me free

I have run through the void
Crossing a thousand villages

Where could I draw breath
Without damaging your scenery?

The nights have flayed me
Like a careless wanderer.

I am simply an insect
Without wings or paws

Scornful serpents are my only fare

Heat crackles upon my roof
The ripe fruit of my flesh is shrinking

Love lies crumpled at my feet.
I would strip myself of all my cares
And wear the dress of consolation only.

Such joy is new to me.

I will take you for my companion
My body is lost in your arms.

But make me insensate as the wind
Which strikes and ravages nature,
Not to make me hate you
But to love you always.

Ghana

Kwesi Brew

A Plea for Mercy

We have come to your shrine to worship –
We the sons of the land.
The naked cowherd has brought
The cows safely home,
And stands silent with his bamboo flute
Wiping the rain from his brow;
As the birds brood in their nests
Awaiting the dawn with unsung melodies;
The shadows crowd on the shores
Pressing their lips against the bosom of the sea;
The peasants home from their labours
Sit by their log fires
Telling tales of long ago.
Why should we the sons of the land
Plead unheeded before your shrine,
When our hearts are full of song
And our lips tremble with sadness?
The little firefly vies with the star,
The log fire with the sun
The water in the calabash
With the mighty Volta.
But we have come in tattered penury
Begging at the door of a Master.

The Search

The past
Is but the cinders
Of the present;
The future
The smoke
That escaped
Into the cloud-bound sky.

Be gentle, be kind my beloved
For words become memories,
And memories tools
In the hands of jesters.
When wise men become silent,
It is because they have read
The palms of Christ
In the face of the Buddha.

So look not for wisdom
And guidance
In their speech, my beloved.
Let the same fire
Which chastened their tongues
Into silence,
Teach us – teach us!

The rain came down,
When you and I slept away
The night's burden of our passions;
Their new-found wisdom
In quick lightning flashes
Revealed the truth
That they had been
The slaves of fools.

Ellis Ayitey Komey

The Change

Your infancy now a wall of memory
In harmattan the locusts filled the sky
Destroying the sweat put into the field
And restless seas shattered canoes
The fisher-folk put to sail by noon.
The impatience in your teens
Yet silent were your dreams
With the fires in your heart
Breaking the mask of innocence.
The evasive solitude in your womb
And the determination of your limbs
With eyes like the soaring eagle
Shattering the glass of ignorance.
Your infancy now a wall of memory
Before this you, like the worms,
Leaning on for vain indecorous dreams
And the cobras with venomous tongues
Licking the tepid blooms of hibiscus.

G. Awoonor-Williams

Songs of Sorrow

Dzogbese Lisa has treated me thus
It has led me among the sharps of the forest
Returning is not possible
And going forward is a great difficulty
The affairs of this world are like the chameleon faeces
Into which I have stepped
When I clean it cannot go.*

I am on the world's extreme corner,
I am not sitting in the row with the eminent
But those who are lucky
Sit in the middle and forget
I am on the world's extreme corner
I can only go beyond and forget.

My people, I have been somewhere
If I turn here, the rain beats me
If I turn there the sun burns me
The firewood of this world
Is for only those who can take heart
That is why not all can gather it.
The world is not good for anybody
But you are so happy with your fate;
Alas! the travellers are back
All covered with debt.

   * Colloquial: It [the faeces] will not go [come off].

Something has happened to me
The things so great that I cannot weep;
I have no sons to fire the gun when I die
And no daughters to wail when I close my mouth
I have wandered on the wilderness
The great wilderness men call life
The rain has beaten me,
And the sharp stumps cut as keen as knives
I shall go beyond and rest.
I have no kin and no brother,
Death has made war upon our house;

And Kpeti's great household is no more,
Only the broken fence stands;
And those who dared not look in his face
Have come out as men.
How well their pride is with them.
Let those gone before take note
They have treated their offspring badly.
What is the wailing for?
Somebody is dead. Agosu himself
Alas! a snake has bitten me
My right arm is broken,
And the tree on which I lean is fallen.

Agosu if you go tell them,
Tell Nyidevu, Kpeti, and Kove
That they have done us evil;
Tell them their house is falling
And the trees in the fence
Have been eaten by termites;
That the martels curse them.
Ask them why they idle there
While we suffer, and eat sand,
And the crow and the vulture
Hover always above our broken fences
And strangers walk over our portion.

Song of War

I shall sleep in white calico;
War has come upon the sons of men
And I shall sleep in calico;
Let the boys go forward,
Kpli and his people should go forward;
Let the white man's guns boom,
We are marching forward;
We all shall sleep in calico.

When we start, the ground shall shake;
The war is within our very huts;
Cowards should fall back
And live at home with the women;
They who go near our wives
While we are away in battle
Shall lose their calabashes when we come.

Where has it been heard before
That a snake has bitten a child
In front of its own mother;
The war is upon us
It is within our very huts
And the sons of men shall fight it
Let the white man's guns boom
And its smoke cover us
We are fighting them to die.

We shall die on the battlefield
We shall like death at no other place,
Our guns shall die with us
And our sharp knives shall perish with us
We shall die on the battlefield.

The Sea Eats the Land at Home

At home the sea is in the town,
Running in and out of the cooking places,
Collecting the firewood from the hearths
And sending it back at night;
The sea eats the land at home.
It came one day at the dead of night,
Destroying the cement walls,
And carried away the fowls,
The cooking-pots and the ladles,
The sea eats the land at home;
It is a sad thing to hear the wails,
And the mourning shouts of the women,
Calling on all the gods they worship,
To protect them from the angry sea.
Aku stood outside where her cooking-pot stood,
With her two children shivering from the cold,
Her hands on her breast,
Weeping mournfully.
Her ancestors have neglected her,
Her gods have deserted her,
It was a cold Sunday morning,
The storm was raging,
Goats and fowls were struggling in the water,
The angry water of the cruel sea;
The lap-lapping of the bark water at the shore,
And above the sobs and the deep and low moans,
Was the eternal hum of the living sea.
It has taken away their belongings
Adena has lost the trinkets which
Were her dowry and her joy,
In the sea that eats the land at home,
Eats the whole land at home.

Lovers' Song

Call her, call her for me, that girl
That girl with the neck like a desert tree
Call her that she and I will lie in one bed.
When you went away
Isn't it seven years?
Shall I fold mine and say I am cheap
Returned unsold from the market
If they marry a woman don't they sleep with her?
Isn't it seven years now since you went away?

The Weaver Bird

The weaver bird built in our house
And laid its eggs on our only tree
We did not want to send it away
We watched the building of the nest
And supervised the egg-laying.
And the weaver returned in the guise of the owner
Preaching salvation to us that owned the house
They say it came from the west
Where the storms at sea had felled the gulls
And the fishers dried their nets by lantern light
Its sermon is the divination of ourselves
And our new horizons limit at its nest
But we cannot join the prayers and answers of the
    communicants.
We look for new homes every day,
For new altars we strive to rebuild
The old shrines defiled by the weaver's excrement.

Easter Dawn

That man died in Jerusalem
And his death demands dawn marchers
From year to year to the sound of bells.
The hymns flow through the mornings
Heard on Calvary this dawn.

       the gods are crying, my father's gods are crying
       for a burial – for a final ritual –
       but they that should build the fallen shrines
       have joined the dawn marchers
       singing their way towards Gethsemane
       where the tear drops of agony still freshen the cactus.

He has risen! Christ has risen!

       the gods cried again from the hut in me
       asking why that prostration has gone unheeded.

The marchers sang of the resurrection
That concerned the hillock of Calvary
Where the ground at the foot of the cross is level.

       the gods cried, shedding
       clayey tears on the calico
       the drink offering had dried up in the harmattan
       the cola-nut is shrivelled
       the yam feast has been eaten by mice
       and the fetish priest is dressing for the Easter
          service.

The resurrection hymns come to me from afar
touching my insides.

       Then the gods cried loudest
       Challenging the hymners.
       They seized their gongs and drums
       And marched behind the dawn marchers
       Seeking their Calvary
       Seeking their tombstones
       And those who refused to replace them
       In the appropriate season.

Jawa Apronti

Funeral

At home Death claims
Two streams from women's eyes
And many day-long dirges;
Gnashes, red eyes and sighs from men,
The wailing of drums and muskets
And a procession of the townsfolk
Impeded
Only if the coffin decides
To take one last look at the home.

But here I see
Three cars in procession.
The first holds three –
A driver chatting gaily with a mate,
And behind them, flowers on a bier.
The second holds five, and the third too.

A procession
Efficiently arranged by the undertaker,
From the brass fittings on the bier
To the looks of sorrow on the mourners' faces.
And Death is escorted
Tearlessly but efficiently
By
Three cars in procession.

Dahomey

Ologoudou

Vespers

Autumnal skies
the sun has smashed his jar of red oil,
on this day of great anger over the earth
I will leave the dainty lettering of the sky
with
this
message heavy as a bobbin of lead
to tell my people what I am told to tell them,
it is the fixed invective of the other shore
and
the heart at this work for the rest of my life,
I shall see no more this sun which totters,
this light which crumples under the slow shadows,
ah!
what are they these things which capsize
in
the sea of my being at the hour of departure?
it is, at the very summit of the soul,
terror before the thousand promises we shall be able to
    keep.

Liberty

The white carcases
of
ships
sought desperately
the visible island with its golden mist,
the native isle of insurrection,
stage at evening of the most tragic adventures,
we were tossed
on the waves of the same sorrow,
and discord
had not yet blown towards us the sands
of
its evidence,
exuberance still reigned over the happy bay,
that day when we made long funerals
for all the things
we had to bury . . .

Nigeria

John Pepper Clark

Olokun*

I love to pass my fingers,
As tide through weeds of the sea.
And wind the tall fern-fronds
Through the strands of your hair
Dark as night that screens the naked moon:

I am jealous and passionate
Like Jehovah, God of the Jews,
And I would that you realize
No greater love had woman
From man than the one I have for you!

But what wakeful eyes of man,
Made of the mud of this earth,
Can stare at the touch of sleep
The sable vehicle of dream
Which indeed is the look of your eyes?

So drunken, like ancient walls
We crumble in heaps at your feet;
And as the good maid of the sea,
Full of rich bounties for men,
You lift us all beggars to your breast.

  * Olokun: goddess of the sea.

Night Rain

What time of night it is
I do not know
Except that like some fish
Doped out of the deep
I have bobbed up bellywise
From stream of sleep
And no cocks crow.
It is drumming hard here
And I suppose everywhere
Droning with insistent ardour upon
Our roof-thatch and shed
And through sheaves slit open
To lightning and rafters
I cannot make out overhead
Great water drops are dribbling
Falling like orange or mango
Fruits showered forth in the wind
Or perhaps I should say so
Much like beads I could in prayer tell
Them on string as they break
In wooden bowls and earthenware
Mother is busy now deploying
About our roomlet and floor.
Although it is so dark
I know her practised step as
She moves her bins, bags, and vats
Out of the run of water
That like ants filing out of the wood
Will scatter and gain possession
Of the floor. Do not tremble then
But turn brothers, turn upon your side
Of the loosening mats
To where the others lie.
We have drunk tonight of a spell
Deeper than the owl's or bat's

That wet of wings may not fly.
Bedraggled upon the *iroko*, they stand
Emptied of hearts, and
Therefore will not stir, no, not
Even at dawn for then
They must scurry in to hide.
So we'll roll over on our back
And again roll to the beat
Of drumming all over the land
And under its ample soothing hand
Joined to that of the sea
We will settle to sleep of the innocent.

The Imprisonment of Obatala*

Those stick-insect figures! they rock the dance
Of snakes, dart after Him daddy-long arms,
Tangle their loping strides to mangrove stance
And He, roped in the tightening pit of alarms
Dangles in His front, full length,
Invincible limbs cramped by love of their strength.

And that mischievous stir, late sown or split
On the way between homestead and stream,
Wells up in pots long stagnant on stilt,
Brims out to where ancestral eyes gleam
Till angry waves dam His track
And caterpillars riding break their back.

One leap upon the charcoal-coloured ass
Swishing ochre urine towards palace and sun,
Kicking impatient tattoo on the grass,
And generations unborn spared the wrong.
But the cry of a child at what it knows not
Evokes trebly there the droop, mud-crack, and clot.

   * Obatala: Yoruba god of creation. This poem was inspired by a
batik showing the ritual imprisonment of the god.

Easter

So death
being the harvest of God
when this breath
has blown uncertain above the sod,
what seed, cast out in turmoil
to sprout, shall in despair
not beat the air
who falls on rock swamp or the yielding soil?

in thrall
mute with the soft pad of sheet
hung up on the wall,
I draw in my hook-feet:
hear the reaper's cry! the rap
of his crook on the door –
but the poor
dupe! opening, shall find bats far gone with my sap.

For Granny (from Hospital)

Tell me, before the ferryman's return,
What was that stirred without your soul,
One night fifteen floods today,
When upon a dugout
Mid pilgrim lettuce on the Niger,
You with a start strained me to breast:
Did you that night in the raucous voice
Of yesterday's rain,
Tumbling down banks of reed
To feed a needless stream,
Then recognize the loud note of quarrels
And endless dark nights of intrigue
In Father's house of many wives?

Or was it wonder at those footless stars
Who in their long translucent fall
Make shallow silten floors
Beyond the pale of muddy waters
Appear more plumbless than the skies?

Ibadan

Ibadan,
            running splash of rust
and gold – flung and scattered
among seven hills like broken
china in the sun.

Fulani Cattle

Contrition twines me like a snake
Each time I come upon the wake
Of your clan,
Undulating along in agony,
You face a stool for mystery:
What secret hope or knowledge,
Locked in your hump away from man,
Imbues you with courage
So mute and fierce and wan
That, not demurring nor kicking,
You go to the house of slaughter?
Can it be in the forging
Of your gnarled and crooked horn
You'd experienced passions far stronger
Than storms which brim up the Niger?
Perhaps, the drover's whip no more
On your balding hind and crest

Arouses shocks of ecstasy:
Or likely the drunken journey
From desert, through grass and forest,
To the hungry towns by the sea
Does call at least for rest –
But will you not first vouchsafe to me,
As true the long knife must prevail,
The patience of even your tail?

Cry of Birth

An echo of childhood stalks before me
like evening shadows on the earth,
rolling back into piquant memory
the anguished cry of my birth;

Out of the caverns of nativity
a voice, I little knew as my own
and thought to have shed with infancy,
returns with a sharpness before unknown.

Poor castaways to this darkling shore,
void out of the sea of eternity
and blind, we catch by reflex horror
an instant glimpse, the guilt of our see:

The souls of men are steeped in stupor
who, tenants upon this wild isle unblest,
sleep on, oblivious of its loud nightmare
with wanton motions bedevilling our breast.

All night, through its long reaches and black
I wander as Io, driven by strange passions,
within and out, and for gadfly have at my back
one harrowing shriek of pain and factions –

It comes ceaseless as from the wilderness!
commingled with the vague cogitation

of the sea, its echo of despair and stress
precedes me like a shade to the horizon.

Abiku*

Coming and going these several seasons,
Do stay out on the baobab tree,
Follow where you please your kindred spirits
If indoors it is not enough for you.
True, it leaks through the thatch
When floods brim the banks,
And the bats and the owls
Often tear in at night through the eaves,
And at harmattan, the bamboo walls
Are ready tinder for the fire
That dries the fresh fish up on the rack.
Still, it's been the healthy stock
To several fingers, to many more will be
Who reach to the sun.
No longer then bestride the threshold
But step in and stay
For good. We know the knife-scars
Serrating down your back and front
Like beak of the sword-fish,
And both your ears, notched
As a bondsman to this house,
Are all relics of your first comings.
Then step in, step in and stay
For her body is tired,
Tired, her milk going sour
Where many more mouths gladden the heart.

* Abiku: a 'spirit child'; one fated to a cycle of early death and
rebirth to the same mother.

A Child Asleep

He who plucked light
From under shade of a tree
Sat so in dust, but in silence,
Passing like a spear clean into
The pith of things. But you,
Graft to an old bombax tree,
Raised on fulness of sap science
Cannot give, breed flies
In the oil of our evening,
Have sat dropsical feeding
On desire: it squashes, like dried
Out ribs of tobacco an old woman
Is turning into snuff you tried
To wreck with stones –
But oh look at what we spies
Have missed! In the sand
Here at our feet already fallen is
Your stool, and how clean
Past our fingers, teasing and
Tugging, you have slumped down
A natal stump, there shed
Distended in the dust – No!
As a primeval shadow
Tumbling head over heels into arms of light.

The Leader

They have felled him to the ground
Who announced home from abroad
Wrestled to a standstill his champion
Cousin the Killer of Cows. Yes,
In all that common
And swamp, pitched piecemeal by storks,

No iguana during a decade of tongues
Could throw or twist him round
While he rallied the race and clan.
Now like an alligator he lies
Trussed up in a house without eyes
And ears:
      Bit of bamboo,
Flung to laggard dogs by drowning
Nearest of kin, has quite locked his jaws.

His Excellency the Masquerader

He serves
To ford between swamp and sand,
He serves!

The bridge stands,
All that stone and steel put together,
It stands;

But bolts drop,
And steel that should be blue
At close grip

Shows brown . . .
And for such service, songs more than
Water and sand:

In Ojoto
So they worship the masks,
Altho' in season –

The masks!
O take off the mask! And behind?
What wind! What straw!

Gabriel Okara

The Snowflakes Sail Gently Down

The snowflakes sail gently
down from the misty eye of the sky
and fall lightly lightly on the
winter-weary elms. And the branches
winter-stripped and nude, slowly
with the weight of the weightless snow
bow like grief-stricken mourners
as white funeral cloth is slowly
unrolled over deathless earth.
And dead sleep stealthily from the
heater rose and closed my eyes with
the touch of silk cotton on water falling.

Then I dreamed a dream
in my dead sleep. But I dreamed
not of earth dying and elms a vigil
keeping. I dreamed of birds, black
birds flying in my inside, nesting
and hatching on oil palms bearing suns
for fruits and with roots denting the
uprooters' spades. And I dreamed the
uprooters tired and limp, leaning on my roots –
their abandoned roots
and the oil palms gave them each a sun.

But on their palms
they balanced the blinding orbs

and frowned with schisms on their
brows – for the suns reached not
the brightness of gold!

Then I awoke. I awoke
to the silently falling snow
and bent-backed elms bowing and
swaying to the winter wind like
white-robed Moslems salaaming at evening
prayer, and the earth lying inscrutable
like the face of a god in a shrine.

Piano and Drums

When at break of day at a riverside
I hear jungle drums telegraphing
the mystic rhythm, urgent, raw
like bleeding flesh, speaking of
primal youth and the beginning,
I see the panther ready to pounce,
the leopard snarling about to leap
and the hunters crouch with spears poised;

And my blood ripples, turns torrent,
topples the years and at once I'm
in my mother's lap a suckling;
at once I'm walking simple
paths with no innovations,
rugged, fashioned with the naked
warmth of hurrying feet and groping hearts
in green leaves and wild flowers pulsing.

Then I hear a wailing piano
solo speaking of complex ways
in tear-furrowed concerto;
of **far-away** lands

and new horizons with
coaxing diminuendo, counterpoint,
crescendo. But lost in the labyrinth
of its complexities, it ends in the middle
of a phrase at a daggerpoint.

And I lost in the morning mist
of an age at a riverside keep
wandering in the mystic rhythm
of jungle drums and the concerto.

Were I to Choose

When Adam broke the stone
and red streams raged down to
gather in the womb,
an angel calmed the storm;

And I, the breath mewed
in Cain, unblinking gaze
at the world without
from the brink of an age

That draws from the groping lips
a breast-muted cry
to thread the years.
(O were I to choose)

And now the close of one
and thirty turns, the world
of bones is Babel, and
the different tongues within
are flames the head
continually burning.

And O of this dark halo
were the tired head free.

And when the harmattan
of days has parched the throat
and skin, and sucked the fever
of the head away,

Then the massive dark
descends, and flesh and bone
are razed. And (O were I
to choose) I'd cheat the worms
and silence seek in stone.

The Mystic Drum

The mystic drum beat in my inside
and fishes danced in the rivers
and men and women danced on land
to the rhythm of my drum

But standing behind a tree
with leaves around her waist
she only smiled with a shake of her head.

Still my drum continued to beat,
rippling the air with quickened
tempo compelling the quick
and the dead to dance and sing
with their shadows –

But standing behind a tree
with leaves around her waist
she only smiled with a shake of her head.

Then the drum beat with the rhythm
of the things of the ground
and invoked the eye of the sky
the sun and the moon and the river gods –
and the trees began to dance,

the fishes turned men
and men turned fishes
and things stopped to grow –

But standing behind a tree
with leaves around her waist
she only smiled with a shake of her head.

And then the mystic drum
in my inside stopped to beat –
and men became men,
fishes became fishes
and trees, the sun and the moon
found their places, and the dead
went to the ground and things began to grow.

And behind the tree she stood
with roots sprouting from her
feet and leaves growing on her head
and smoke issuing from her nose
and her lips parted in her smile
turned cavity belching darkness.

Then, then I packed my mystic drum
and turned away; never to beat so loud any more.

Adhiambo

I hear many voices
like it's said a madman hears;
I hear trees talking
like it's said a medicine man hears.

Maybe I'm a madman,
I'm a medicine man.

Maybe I'm mad,
for the voices are luring me,

urging me from the midnight
moon and the silence of my desk
to walk on wave crests across a sea.

Maybe I'm a medicine man
hearing talking saps,
seeing behind trees;
but who's lost his powers
of invocation.

But the voices and the trees
are now name-spelling and one figure
silence-etched across
the moonface is walking, stepping
over continents and seas.

And I raised my hand –
my trembling hand, gripping
my heart as handkerchief
and waved and waved – and waved –
but she turned her eyes away.

Spirit of the Wind

The storks are coming now –
white specks in the silent sky.
They had gone north seeking
fairer climes to build their homes
when here was raining.

They are back with me now –
Spirits of the wind,
beyond the gods' confining
hands they go north and west and east,
instinct guiding.

But willed by the gods
I'm sitting on this rock

watching them come and go
from sunrise to sundown, with the spirit
urging within.

And urging a red pool stirs,
and each ripple is
the instinct's vital call,
a desire in a million cells
confined.

O God of the gods and me,
shall I not heed
this prayer-bell call, the noon
angelus, because my stork is caged
in Singed Hair and Dark Skin?

One Night at Victoria Beach

The wind comes rushing from the sea,
the waves curling like mambas strike
the sands and recoiling hiss in rage
washing the Aladuras' feet pressing hard
on the sand and with eyes fixed hard
on what only hearts can see, they shouting
pray, the Aladuras pray; and coming
from booths behind, compelling highlife
forces ears; and car lights startle pairs
arm in arm passing washer-words back
and forth like haggling sellers and buyers –

Still they pray, the Aladuras pray
with hands pressed against their hearts
and their white robes pressed against
their bodies by the wind; and drinking
palm-wine and beer, the people boast
at bars at the beach. Still they pray.

They pray, the Aladuras pray
to what only hearts can see while dead
fishermen long dead with bones rolling
nibbled clean by nibbling fishes, follow
four dead cowries shining like stars
into deep sea where fishes sit in judgement;
and living fishermen in dark huts
sit round dim lights with Babalawo
throwing their souls in four cowries
on sand, trying to see tomorrow.

Still, they pray, the Aladuras* pray
to what only hearts can see behind
the curling waves and the sea, the stars
and the subduing unanimity of the sky
and their white bones beneath the sand.

And standing dead on dead sands,
I felt my knees touch living sands –
but the rushing wind killed the budding words.

* Aladuras: a Christian sect addicted to ritual bathing.

Frank Aig-Imoukhuede

One Wife for One Man

I done try go church, I done go for court
Dem all day talk about di 'new culture':
Dem talk about 'equality', dem mention 'divorce'
Dem holler am so-tay my ear nearly cut;
     One wife be for one man.

My fader before my fader get him wife borku.*
E no' get equality palaver; he live well
For he be oga† for im own house.
But dat time done pass before white man come
Wit 'im
     One wife for one man,

Tell me how una‡ woman no go make yanga§
Wen'e know say na'im only dey.
Suppose say – make God no 'gree – 'e no born at all?§§
A'tell you dat man bin dey crazy wey start
     One wife for one man.

Jus' tell me how one wife fit do one man;
How go fit stay all time for him house
For time when belleh done kommot.
How many pickin', self, one woman fit born
     Wen one wife be for one man?

* borku = plenty. † oga = master or Lord. ‡ una = variation of 'your'. § yanga = vanity, pride, and perversity. §§ she has no children.

Suppose, self, say na so-so woman your wife dey born
Suppose your wife sabe book, no'sabe make chop;
Den, how you go tell man make'e no' go out
Sake of dis divorce? Bo, dis culture na waya O!
      Wen one wife be for one man.

Michael Echeruo

Sophia

Left hand is God's hand
Devil's hand across chaos
When Eve began
Was hers in Eden farm
Through cats' tiger's fur
Through Adam's core.

Multiply and till the earth
Plough on virgin land is temptation.

And there was a fountain
Of rain and grain.
Force fountain down gorge
Into valley of shoots
Is not spilling
But will not bloom on Martha
Or *Vita Nuova*

Eat apples by the left hand,
Much sweeter. Right hand
Is Right's hand, bitter,
Sweet gorgeless Sophia.

Melting Pot

It is dark, now, and grave

This bowl of a world
That rings me round and round
And will not let me marvel enough
At this dull sky
At the ignorance of these men
Who cannot know what chance can do

I shudder
Before this bowl of a world,
At this dull sky.

Will they not, all of them,
Call me names when they hear
Their blind man of this city
Stumbled on an udara underfoot
And lost it in the search for more?

Wish they could see half
What my eyes see, or know
Half what I know!
The Century's blind man!

Easter Penitence

O crucible
O furnace
        from the darkness and delirium
        the emptiness of another ecstasy.

O crucifix
O chalice
        for the remnants and fragrance
        the heartburn of Easter sacrifice.

O sunrise!
>   Bird of glory at dawn
>   Bird of wonder at dawn
>   Reigning for ever in glory

Pilgrim of Emmaus
speaking to him in their tongue
>   arguing
And he answered only in a word.
>   *Raca*!
  O thou God!

  Speak again.
>   *Raca*!
>   left thy child in the fog
>   left thy bug in the sun
  O thou God!

>   *miserere.*
oil water and light
crucible O, and the crucifix.
>   O God.

Christopher Okigbo

From *Lament of the Lavender Mist*

Love Apart

The moon has ascended between us
Between two pines
That bow to each other

Love with the moon has ascended
Has fed on our solitary stems

And we are now shadows
That cling to each other
But kiss the air only.

Eight poems from *Heavensgate*

Overture

Before you, mother Idoto,
naked I stand,
before your watery presence,
a prodigal,

leaning on an oilbean,
lost in your legend. . . .

Under your power wait I
        on barefoot,
watchman for the watchword
        at heavensgate;

out of the depths my cry
give ear and hearken.

Eyes Watch the Stars

Eyes open on the beach,
eyes open, of the prodigal;
upward to heaven shoot
where stars will fall from.

Which secret I have told into no ear;
    into a dughole to hold,
    not to drown with –
Which secret I have planted into beachsand;

        now breaks
salt-white surf on the stones and me,
    and lobsters and shells in
    iodine smell –
    maid of the salt-emptiness,
    sophisticreamy, native,

whose secret I have covered up with beachsand.

    Shadow of rain
    over sunbeaten beach,
    shadow of rain
    over man with woman.

Water Maid

Bright
with the armpit dazzle of a lioness,
she answers,

wearing white light about her;
and the waves escort her,
my lioness,
crowned with moonlight.

So brief her presence –
match-flare in wind's breath –
so brief with mirrors around me.

Downward . . .
the waves distil her:
gold crop
sinking ungathered.

Watermaid of the salt emptiness,
grown are the ears of the secret.

Transition

Drop of dew on green bowl fostered
on leaf green bowl grows under the lamp

       without flesh or colour;

under the lamp into stream of
       song, streamsong,
in flight into the infinite –
       a blinded heron
thrown against the infinite –
       where solitude
weaves her interminable mystery
       under the lamp.

The moonman has gone under the sea:
the singer has gone under the shade.

Sacrifice

Thundering drums and cannons
in palm grove:
the spirit is in ascent.

I have visited,
on palm beam imprinted
my pentagon –

I have visited, the prodigal. . . .

In palm grove
long drums and cannons:
the spirit in the ascent.

Passion Flower

And the flower weeps
        unbruised,
Lacrimae Christi,

For him who was silenced;

        whose advent
dumb bells in the dim light celebrate
        with wine song:

Messiah will come again,
After the argument in heaven;
Messiah will come again,
Lumen mundi. . . .

Fingers of penitence
bring
to a palm grove
vegetable offering
with five
fingers of chalk.

Lustra

So would I to the hills again
so would I
to where springs the fountain
there to draw from
and to hilltop clamber
body and soul
whitewashed in the moondew
there to see from

So would I from my eye the mist
so would I
through moonmist to hilltop
there for the cleansing

Here is a new-laid egg
here a white hen at midterm.

Bridge

I am standing above you and tide
        above the noontide,
Listening to the laughter of waters
        that do not know why:

Listening to incense. . . .

I am standing above the noontide
        with my head above it,
Under my feet float the waters:
        tide blows them under.

Four poems from *Limits*

Siren (& the mortar is not yet dry . . .)

1

Suddenly becoming talkative
      like weaverbird
Summoned at offside of
        dream remembered

Between sleep and waking,

I hang up my egg-shells
To you of palm grove,
Upon whose bamboo towers hang
Dripping with yesterupwine

A tiger mask and nude spear. . . .

Queen of the damp half-light,
      I have had my cleansing,
Emigrant with airborne nose,
        The he-goat-on-heat.

2

For he was a shrub among the poplars
Needing more roots
More sap to grow to sunlight
Thirsting for sunlight

A low growth among the forest.

Into the soul
Them selves extended their branches
Into the moments of each living hour
Feeling for audience

Straining thin among the echoes;

138

And out of the solitude
Voice and soul with selves unite
Riding the echoes

Horsemen of the apocalypse

And crowned with one self
The name displays its foliage,
Hanging low

A green cloud above the forest.

3

Banks of reed.
Mountains of broken bottles.

    & the mortar is not yet dry. . . .

Silent the footfall
    soft as cat's paw,
Sandalled in velvet,
    in fur
        So we must go,
Wearing evemist against the shoulders,
Trailing sun's dust sawdust of combat,
With brand burning out at hand-end.

    & the mortar is not yet dry. . . .

        Then we must sing
Tongue-tied without name or audience,
Making harmony among the branches.

And this is the crisis-point,
The twilight moment between
        sleep and waking;
And voice that is reborn transpires
Not thro' pores in the flesh
        but the soul's backbone

Hurry on down
        through the high-arched gate –
Hurry on down
        little stream to the lake;
Hurry on down –
        through the cinder market
Hurry on down
        in the wake of the dream;
Hurry on down –
        To rockpoint of CABLE
        To pull by the rope
        The big white elephant. . . .

    & the mortar is not yet dry
    & the mortar is not yet dry. . . .

& the dream wakes
    & the voice fades
In the damp half-light,
    Like a shadow,

Not leaving a mark.

4

An image insists
    from the flag-pole of the heart,
The image distracts
    with the cruelty of the rose. . . .

    My lioness,
(No shield is lead-plate against you)
Wound me with your seaweed face,
    Blinded like a strongroom.

Distances of your
    armpit-fragrance
Turn chloroform,
    enough for my patience –

When you have finished,
& done up my stitches,
Wake me near the altar,
      & this poem will be finished.

Two poems from *Distances*

1

From flesh into phantom,
on the horizontal stone:

I was the sole witness to my homecoming ...

Serene lights on the other balcony –
redolent fountains, bristling with signs.
But what does my divine rejoicing hold?
A bowl of incense? A nest of fireflies?

I was the sole witness to my homecoming ...

And in the inflorescence of the white chamber,
a voice, from very far away, chanted, and the chamber
   descanted
the birthday of earth, paddling me home through
some dark labyrinth, from laughter to the dream.

Miner into my solitude, incarnate
voice of the dream, you will go,
with me as your chief acolyte,
again into the ant-hole ...

I was the sole witness to my homecoming ...

2

Death lay in ambush,
that evening in that island;
and the voice sought its echo,
that evening in that island,

and the eye lost its light,
and the light lost its shadow.

And the wind, eternal suitor of dead leaves,
unrolled his bandages to the finest swimmer . . .

And it was an evening without flesh or skeleton;
an evening with no silver bells to its tale;
without lanterns; without buntings;
and it was an evening without age or memory –

for we are talking of such commonplace things,
and on the brink of such great events –
and in the freezing tuberoses of the white
chamber, eyes that had lost their animal
colour – havoc of incandescent rays –
pinned me, cold to the marble stretcher,
        until my eyes lost their blood,
        and the blood lost its odour;
and the everlasting fire from the oblong window
forgot the taste of ash in the air's marrow . . .

Anguish and solitude . . .
Smothered, my scattered
cry, the dancers,
lost among their own
snares; the faces,
the hands, held captive;
the interspaces
reddening with blood . . .

And behind them all,
in smock of white cotton,
Death herself,
the chief celebrant,
in a cloud of incense,
paring her fingernails . . .

At her feet roll their heads like cut fruits;
about her fall
their severed members, numerous as locusts.

Like split wood left to dry,
the dismembered joints
of the ministrants pile high.

She bathes her knees in the blood of attendants,
her smock in the entrails of the ministrants . . .

Come Thunder

Now that the triumphant march has entered the last
    street corners,
Remember, O dancers, the thunder among the clouds . .

Now that the laughter, broken in two, hangs
    tremulous between the teeth,
Remember, O dancers, the lightning beyond the earth . . .

The smell of blood already floats in the lavender-mist
    of the afternoon.
The death sentence lies in ambush along the
    corridors of power;
And a great fearful thing already tugs at the cables of
    the open air,
A nebula immense and immeasurable, a night of
    deep waters –
An iron dream unnamed and unprintable, a path of stone.

The drowsy heads of the pods in barren farmlands
    witness it,
The homesteads abandoned in this century's brush
    fire witness it:
The myriad eyes of deserted corn cobs in burning
    barns witness it:
Magic birds with the miracle of lightning flash on their
    feathers . . .

The arrows of God tremble at the gates of light,
The drums of curfew pander to a dance of death;

And the secret thing in its heaving
Threatens with iron mask
The last lighted torch of the century . . .

Wole Soyinka

Telephone Conversation

The price seemed reasonable, location
Indifferent. The landlady swore she lived
Off premises. Nothing remained
But self-confession. 'Madam,' I warned,
'I hate a wasted journey – I am African.'
Silence. Silenced transmission of
Pressurized good-breeding. Voice, when it came,
Lipstick coated, long gold-rolled
Cigarette-holder pipped. Caught I was, foully.
'HOW DARK?' ... I had not misheard. ... 'ARE YOU LIGHT
OR VERY DARK?' Button B. Button A. Stench
Of rancid breath of public hide-and-speak.
Red booth. Red pillar-box. Red double-tiered
Omnibus squelching tar. It *was* real! Shamed
By ill-mannered silence, surrender
Pushed dumbfoundment to beg simplification.
Considerate she was, varying the emphasis –
'ARE YOU DARK? OR VERY LIGHT?' Revelation came.
'You mean – like plain or milk chocolate?'
Her assent was clinical, crushing in its light
Impersonality. Rapidly, wave-length adjusted,
I chose. 'West African sepia' – and as afterthought,
'Down in my passport.' Silence for spectroscopic
Flight of fancy, till truthfulness clanged her accent
Hard on the mouthpiece. 'WHAT'S THAT?' conceding
'DON'T KNOW WHAT THAT IS.' 'Like brunette.'

'THAT'S DARK, ISN'T IT?' 'Not altogether.
Facially, I am brunette, but madam, you should see
The rest of me. Palm of my hand, soles of my feet
Are a peroxide blonde. Friction, caused—
Foolishly madam — by sitting down, has turned
My bottom raven black — One moment madam!' — sensing
Her receiver rearing on the thunderclap
About my ears — 'Madam,' I pleaded, 'wouldn't you
    rather
See for yourself?'

Death in the Dawn

Traveller, you must set out
At dawn. And wipe your feet upon
The dog-nose wetness of the earth.

Let sunrise quench your lamps. And watch
Faint brush pricklings in the sky light
Cottoned feet to break the early earthworm
On the hoe. Now shadows stretch with sap
Not twilight's death and sad prostration.
This soft kindling, soft receding breeds
Racing joys and apprehensions for
A naked day. Burdened hulks retract,
Stoop to the mist in faceless throng
To wake the silent markets — swift, mute
Processions on grey byways. . . . On this
Counterpane, it was —
Sudden winter at the death
Of dawn's lone trumpeter. Cascades
Of white feather-flakes . . . but it proved
A futile rite. Propitiation sped
Grimly on, before.
The right foot for joy, the left, dread

And the mother prayed, Child
May you never walk
When the road waits, famished.

Traveller, you must set forth
At dawn.
I promise marvels of the holy hour
Presages as the white cock's flapped
Perverse impalement – as who would dare
The wrathful wings of man's Progression. . . .

But such another wraith! Brother,
Silenced in the startled hug of
Your invention – is this mocked grimace
This closed contortion – I?

Massacre, October '66

Written in Tegel

Shards of sunlight touch me here
Shredded in willows. Through stained-glass
Fragments on the lake I sought to reach
A mind at silt-bed

The lake stayed cold
I swam in an October flush of dying leaves
The gardener's labour flew in seasoned scrolls
Lettering the wind

Swept from painted craft
A mockery of waves remarked this idyll sham
I trod on acorns; each shell's detonation
Aped the skull's uniqueness.

Came sharper reckoning –
This favoured food of hogs cannot number high
As heads still harshly crop to whirlwinds
I have briefly fled

The oak rains a hundred more
A kind confusion to arithmetics of death:
Time to watch autumn the removal man
Dust down rare canvases

To let a loud resolve of passion
Fly to a squirrel, burnished light and copper fur
A distant stance without the lake's churchwindows
And for a stranger, love.

A host of acorns fell, silent
As they are silenced all, whose laughter
Rose from such indifferent paths, oh God
They are not strangers all

Whose desecration mocks the word
Of peace – *salaam aleikun* – not strangers any
Brain of thousands pressed asleep to pig fodder –
Shun pork the unholy – cries the priest.

I borrow seasons of an alien land
In brotherhood of ill, pride of race around me
Strewn in sunlit shards. I borrow alien lands
To stay the season of a mind.

Civilian and Soldier

My apparition rose from the fall of lead,
Declared, 'I'm a civilian.' It only served
To aggravate your fright. For how could I
Have risen, a being of this world, in that hour
Of impartial death! And I thought also: nor is
Your quarrel of this world.

                    You stood still
For both eternities, and oh I heard the lesson
Of your training sessions, cautioning –
Scorch earth behind you, do not leave
A dubious neutral to the rear. Reiteration
Of my civilian quandry, burrowing earth
From the lead festival of your more eager friends
Worked the worse on your confusion, and when
You brought the gun to bear on me, and death
Twitched me gently in the eye, your plight
And all of you came clear to me.

                  I hope some day
Intent upon my trade of living, to be checked
In stride by *your* apparition in a trench,
Signalling, I am a soldier. No hesitation then
But I shall shoot you clean and fair
With meat and bread, a gourd of wine
A bunch of breasts from either arm, and that
Lone question – do you friend, even now, know
What it is all about?

Prisoner

Grey, to the low grass cropping
Slung, wet-lichened, wisps from such
Smoke heaviness, elusive of thin blades
Curl inward to the earth, breed
The grey hours,
And days, and years, for do not
The wise grey temples we must build
To febrile years, here begin, not
In tears and ashes, but on the sad mocking
Threads, compulsive of the hour?

In the desert wildness, when, lone cactus,
Cannibal was his love – even amidst the
Crag and gorge, the leap and night-tremors
Even as the potsherd stayed and the sandstorm
Fell – intimations came.

In the whorled centre of the storm, a threnody
But not from this. For that far companion,
Made sudden stranger when the wind slacked
And the centre fell, grief. And the stricken
Potsherd lay, disconsolate – intimations then

But not from these. He knew only
Sudden seizure. And time conquest
Bound him helpless to each grey essence.

Nothing remained if pains and longings
Once, once set the walls. Sadness
Closed him, rootless, lacking cause.

I Think it Rains

I think it rains
That tongues may loosen from the parch
Uncleave roof-tops of the mouth, hang
Heavy with knowledge.

I saw it raise
The sudden cloud, from ashes. Settling
They joined in a ring of grey; within
The circling spirit.

O it must rain
These closures on the mind, binding us
In strange despairs, teaching
Purity of sadness.

And how it beats
Skeined transparencies on wings
Of our desires, searing dark longings
In cruel baptisms.

Rain-reeds, practised in
The grace of yielding, yet unbending
From afar, this, your conjugation with my earth
Bares crouching rocks.

Season

Rust is ripeness, rust
And the wilted corn-plume;

Pollen is mating-time when swallows
Weave a dance
Of feathered arrows
Thread corn-stalks in winged
Streaks of light. And, we loved to hear
Spliced phrases of the wind, to hear
Rasps in the field, where corn leaves
Pierce like bamboo slivers.

Now, garnerers we,
Awaiting rust on tassels, draw
Long shadows from the dusk, wreathe
Dry thatch in woodsmoke. Laden stalks
Ride the germ's decay – we await
The promise of the rust.

Night

Your hand is heavy, Night, upon my brow,
I bear no heart mercuric like the clouds, to dare
Exacerbation from your subtle plough.

Woman as a clam, on the sea's crescent
I saw your jealous eye quench the sea's
Fluorescence, dance on the pulse incessant

Of the waves. And I stood, drained
Submitting like the sands, blood and brine
Coursing to the roots. Night, you rained

Serrated shadows through dank leaves
Till, bathed in warm suffusion of your dappled cells
Sensations pained me, faceless, silent as night thieves.

Hide me now, when night children haunt the earth
I must hear none! These misted calls will yet
Undo me; naked, unbidden, at Night's muted birth.

*Abiku**

In vain your bangles cast
Charmed circles at my feet
I am Abiku, calling for the first
And the repeated time.

Must I weep for goats and cowries
For palm oil and the sprinkled ash?
Yams do not sprout in amulets
To earth Abiku's limbs.

So when the snail is burnt in his shell,
Whet the heated fragment, brand me
Deeply on the breast. You must know him
When Abiku calls again.

I am the squirrel teeth, cracked
The riddle of the palm. Remember
This, and dig me deeper still into
The god's swollen foot.

Once and the repeated time, ageless
Though I puke; and when you pour
Libations, each finger points me near
The way I came, where

The ground is wet with mourning
White dew suckles flesh-birds
Evening befriends the spider, trapping
Flies in wind-froth;

Night, and Abiku sucks the oil
From lamps. Mothers! I'll be the
Suppliant snake coiled on the doorstep
Yours the killing cry.

The ripest fruit was saddest;
Where I crept, the warmth was cloying.
In the silence of webs, Abiku moans, shaping
Mounds from the yolk.

* Abiku: see p. 91 n.

Aig Higo

Ritual Murder

No animals will live
Rivers will be dry
The rotund seal will snap
Eager vultures will show
The sacred spring is stained red with lust

Our seedlings bake on the rocks
Fresh leaves wither in pain
The black-robed virgins ate here, hot-eyed,
Breathing agony, prowling with parted lips.

I hear their voodoo dance to soothe
And melt the hurt strains of their trance.
They've come to mourn the spectral eunuchs of the shrine.

Hidesong

    I struck tomorrow square in the face
Yesterday groaned and said,
        'Please mind your steps today.'
    I left them swimming with today.

        Hidesong
        Birdsong
        Unto my soul
        What funeral pyre rejects your bones?

My spider soul is spinning
Spinning
    Spinning endlessly.

Scarabwise I tow my days along
Alone I tow my death along.

Pol N Ndu

udude
(at cock crow)

grave number twenty-four
red axe forged from last burials
of twenty-three corpses in me:
Okpoko

horn-man call,
nude queens low in chant
far from lay-men
far from grasshoppers
trembling at your charged incantations:
Mmanwu

transmitting dead-land rumbles
in diction computed
at first cock-crow:
Udude

raw-material un-human
in invincible cocoon
explaining miracle photogropic:
burst-balloon

time-keeper of innumerable sperms
frantic in vibration
to chaotic chemistry:
I win!

The purest victory of all. . . .
victory of vision
      of visitation
      of creation
perfect without contribution,
new-born fire-intricate
delicate because sharp
fierce in steadiness

I yearn

Okogbule Wonodi

Planting

Lights on the shore
that was our port,
that was our fort;

and wind swaying scenes
that we know
        aside,
while the sea shells
stand aside,
season aside to make
mouths at us

birds on the stems,
pecking at the scare-crows
to call the farmer home,
who then shall follow,
with white shirts
the dance of his father
as tractors bite down
the yam god
and the squirrels skip about
making faces at us?

Stand
You that hate not
and praise not
these shifting scenes,
season and blow
the horn of *Rebisi*;*

  * Rebisi: ancestral god of the Diobu people.

that we,
who shall hear
the cock at night
and see the red snake at day
and they that shall follow,
bow not
when the sea shells
season aside
making mouths at us.

Salute to Icheke

When did I cease to be
the bird that I have been;
was it that I have fallen
sullen at midstream,
or immersed earthwise
I have gone dusty with wives
that cook for men with irregularities
between their thighs?

    No father.
I am yet your harp;
tune me but fingerly
and my strings will echo
songs of my inside.

I am your right hand,
I will mend your barn
and girdle my breath
for after this harvest
there's the visit adults
and orphans will call
from windowless houses;
then will come the test
of my planting songs.

Romanus Egudu

The Conqueror's Sword

Give it to right?
no, the sharpness of a knife
is in the might of the arm;
so the sword to might;
right can grovel
and lie in defeat.

Then the soil will be blood-bathed;
It will be fertilized thereof,
and in April shoots of tears
will sprout, and after,
we sing the dirge of innocence.

Then shall we see the low
under a weight, his basket-load
of the high;
he will grow down and down,
lower and lower, till he attains
the height of mother earth.

He will sound a horn of triumph,
for he can grow no less, he fears
neither a slip nor fall,
being so highly down,
being so roundly flat.

Cameroons

Mbella Sonne Dipoko

Our Life

An ailing bird over the desert made its agony
A song blown through the air
As at the oasis
Drawers of water said
How low it flies oh how touching its song

The winged hope that proved to be a dream
(Masked our destiny with a black hood)

As in the cities we said the same prayers
As in the villages we espoused ancestral myths
Transmitting our frustration our life our mortality
To the young country of tomorrow and day after tomorrow
Flattering ourselves with the charity of the blood-donor's
   love.

Pain

All was quiet in this park
Until the wind, like a gasping messenger, announced
The tyrant's coming.
Then did the branches talk in agony.

You remember that raging storm?
In their fear despairing flowers nevertheless held bouquets
   to the grim king;

Meteors were the tassels of his crown
More like branches that only spoke when the storm
  menaced
We cried in agony as we fell
Slashed by the cold blade of an invisible sword.

Mutilated our limbs were swept away by the rain
But not our blood;
Indelible, it stuck on the walls
Like wild gum on tree-trunks.

Exile

In silence
The overloaded canoe leaves our shores

But who are these soldiers in camouflage,
These clouds going to rain in foreign lands?

The night is losing its treasures
The future seems a myth
Warped on a loom worked by lazy hands.

But perhaps all is not without some good for us
As from the door of a shack a thousand miles away
The scaly hand of a child takes in greeting
The long and skinny fingers of the rain.

Patrice Kayo

Song of the Initiate

All the wives of my father
        pulled my mother to bits
But their children cannot dance
It is I who have taken my father's stool
And my mother has become queen
All the wives of my father my wives
        and servants of my mother.

The mother of those who cannot dance
        has never borne children
Her children are nothing but epileptics
        The initiate alone with the chief.

If only I were a river!
I would roll down all silvery
And in the compound of the non-initiate
        I would become a swamp.

I am only a dealer in pigs
        and in chickens
But if you have any pearls or little bells
        I will buy them.
The only son alone
Is sure of his father's stool.
The panther's child does not fear the night
I can dance all the dances
And my mother eats nothing but the flesh of sparrowhawks.

Congo (Brazzaville)

Tchicaya U Tam'si

Brush-fire

The fire the river that's to say
the sea to drink following the sand
the feet the hands
within the heart to love
this river that lives in me repeoples me
only to you I said around the fire

my race
it flows here and there a river
the flames are the looks
of those who brood upon it
I said to you
my race
remembers
the taste of bronze drunk hot.

Dance to the Amulets

Come over here
our grass is rich
come you fawns

gestures and stabs of sickly hands
curving then unripping of conception
one – who? – you shape my fate
come you fawns

over here the suppleness of mornings
and the blood masked here
and the rainbow-coloured dream the rope at the neck
come over here

our grass is rich here
my first coming
was the harsh explosion of a flint
solitude
my mother promised me to light.

Still Life

I was playing
when my dead sister
my grandfather hung
a great fish
on a tree before our gate.

We adored aubergines
I devoured the little gourds
but I had to fast

also I cried with hunger,
if I tell you
my father does not know my mother's name
I am the witness of my age
I have often seen
carcases in the air
where my blood burns.

A Mat to Weave

he came to deliver the secret of the sun
and wanted to write the poem of his life

why crystals in his blood
why globules in his laughter

his soul was ready
when someone called him
dirty wog

still he is left with the gentle act of his laughter
and the giant tree with a living cleft
what was that country where he lived a beast
behind the beasts before behind the beasts

his stream was the safest of cups
because it was of bronze
because it was his living flesh

it was then that he said to himself
no my life is not a poem

here is the tree here is the water here are the stones
and then the priest of the future

it is better to love wine
and rise in the morning
he was advised

but no more birds in the tenderness of mothers
dirty wog
he is the younger brother of fire

the bush begins here
and the sea is no more than the memory of gulls
all standing upright tooth-to-tooth
against the spume of a deadly dance
the tree was the leafiest
the bark of the tree was the tenderest
after the forest was burnt what more to say

why was there absinthe in the wine
why restore in the hearts
the crocodiles the canoers
and the wave of the stream

the grains of sand between the teeth
is it thus that one breaks the world
no
no
his stream was the gentlest of cups
the safest
it was his most living flesh

here begins the poem of his life
he was trained in a school
he was trained in a studio
and he saw roads planted with sphinxes

still he is left with the soft arch of his laughter
then the tree then the water then the leaves

that is why you will see him
the marching canoers have raised once more
against the haulers of french cotton
their cries
this flight is a flight of doves

the leeches did not know the bitterness
of this blood
in the purest of cups

dirty gollywog
behold my congolese head

it is the purest of cups.

Three poems from *Epitomé*

A bouquet of faded flowers in my letterbox . . .

> I was naked for the first kiss of my mother
> I was naked before Sammy and before men

I would be cold already
without this taste of black salt
in your black blood

I have the claws of a woman in my flesh
I bleed for her delight in love
But hide from me the image of her god
that fakir whose grin desalts my soul
and let the ferns
hold in the earth
the freshness of a patch of violent water.

These flowers in my letterbox, I cross my fingers to caress them
and the conscience of the world is silent with me over the drama
of Léopoldville – I spit into the Seine like all good poets.

What do I want with a thousand stars in broad
    daylight
the rapt surrealist
in one of them at midnight
has blessed my crazy reason

My reason is the memory of a levitation
it knits a blue stocking for the violated night
it kindles hell in the black flames it ends
the purification of my sinful swan
which once fixed a halo of pollen

on the head of a lustful black crab
my reason makes me difficult and faithless
in the abstract of my passion.

My prick is not even a root of the tree,
to speak as that tree rustles
would give a rustic perfume
to the game of my flight
and put less blood on the hands of my quest.

The disasters unfold in silence
as one loved them in childhood memory
and a grey rain serves all our dreams
forcing me to become a forger
and holy assassin
despite the equinox
despite myself
despite the sorcery of the smiles
of my obedient black brothers

And then
what would you have me say of this silence
squatting beside my own conscience?

They give you what they have eaten and what they have not
known how to keep. The shadow, like them, had a certain
reticence.
I am full of spite with the sun.

You must be from my country
I see it by the tick
of your soul around the eyelashes
and besides you dance when you are sad
you must be from my country

Keep moving time is waiting to seduce us
learn from this that the oil in your lamp
is really my blood brimming up
and that, if it overflows, you mustn't light your lamp
we must have a dark corner somewhere
for our ancient orisons

All of us from the same umbilical cord
But who knows where we fetch
our awkward heads

Often the silences
reeking of iodine ravage us
with lecherous resolves
for my beardless conscience
ravage us alone.

The Scorner

I drink to your glory my god
You who have made me so sad
You have given me a people who are not distillers of gin

What wine shall I drink to your jubilate
In this country which has no vines
In this desert all the bushes are of cactus
Shall I take their crop of flowers
for flames of the burning bush of your desire
Tell me in what Egypt my people's feet lie chained

Christ I laugh at your sadness
O my sweet Christ
Thorn for thorn
We have a common crown of thorns
I will be converted because you tempt me
Joseph comes to me
I suck already the breast of the Virgin your mother
I count more than your one Judas on my fingers
My eyes lie to my soul
Where the world is a lamb your pascal lamb – Christ
I will waltz to the tune of your slow sadness.

Jean-Baptiste Tati

News of my Mother

I am now very high upon the tree of the seasons;
Far below I see the firm earth of the past.
When the fields opened themselves to the flow of seed
Before the baobab took aim at a flight of birds
With the first call of the sun,
It was your footsteps which sang around me:
A shower of bells chiming with my ablutions.
I am now very high upon the tree of the seasons.
Know by this fifteenth day of the moon
It is these tears – up till now –
Which fill your absence,
Which lighten drop by drop your image
Too heavy on my pupil;
Each night I waken drenched through with your pain
Even as if you lived in me again.

Liberty

The storm sets free a myriad of insects
Locked in the belly of the earth;
They think the hour has come to undertake
Ascent of the Sun-Mountain
And their dream stifles in the swallow's beak.
Each day I guard my life
I cut back a shoot of dreams

I sever every filament of vision
Bred in the fertile straw of night.
And all these parasites go to feed the wind ...
Thus noon burns up a thousand dreams
When the vertical sun speaks its clear syllables;
In the village they are beating the drum of Liberty
Ready to burst it;
But remember that man who dances on
With naked feet
By pathways where the thorns still cry out
With peevishness.

Congo (Kinshasa)

Antoine-Roger Bolamba

Portrait

I have my gri-gri
         gri-gri
         gri-gri
my calm bounding awake
clings to the wavy limbs of the Congo
never a stormy passage for my heart
bombarded with glowing oriflammes
I think of my silver necklace
become a hundred isles of silence
I admire the obstinate patience
of the okapi
bluebird battered in the open sky
what shipwreck
plunges it to the gulf of nothingness
nothingness empty of nightly entreaties

Ah! the broken resolutions
ah! the screaming follies
let my fate fall upon its guardians
they are three villains

I say three in counting 1 2 3
who dim the ancestral mirror
but you fugitive image
I will see you on the height of dizzy anger
wait while I put on my brow my mask of blood
and soon you will see
my tongue flutter like a banner.

A Fistful of News

The hills hunch their backs
and leap above the marshes
that wash about the calabash
of the Great Soul

Rumours of treason spread
like burning swords
the veins of the earth
swell with nourishing blood
the earth bears
towns villages hamlets
forests and woods
peopled with monsters horned and tentacled
their long manes are the mirror of the Sun

they are those who when night has come
direct the regiments of bats
and who sharpen their arms
upon the stone of horror.

the souls of the guilty
float in the currents of air
on the galleys of disaster
paying no heed to the quarrels of the earthbound
with fangs of fire
they tear from the lightning its diamond heart.

Surely the scorn is a gobbet of smoking flesh
surely the spirits recite the rosary of vengeance
but like the black ear of wickedness
they have never understood a single word
of the scorpion's obscure tongue:
stubbornness

nor the anger of the snake-wizard
nor the violence of the throwing-knife
can do anything against it.

Emmanuel Boundzeki-Dongala

Fantasy Under the Moon
(Blues for a muted trumpet)

I climbed towards you on a ray of moonlight
that filtered through a hole in my straw-thatched house
When I had reached the smiling arch of your mouth among
   the stars
you came to me
open under the sea of your body the heaving wave under
   my body
my heart beating to the rythm of yours moving to the
   rythm of your tribe the people of the mountain;
your serpent form writhing beneath mine
I sucked your cobra's poison from your broken lips
and my fever mounted like a sickness.

I visited last night our banana grove of the first time.
When I reached those great sombre aisles
under which we pressed each other beyond your mother's
   knowledge
under the teasing trumpet of thirsty mosquitoes
the circle of my arms about your shadow your phantom
all at once hung emptier than the rope of a wine-tapper
embracing the palm tree.

I don't know why that large cloud crossing the moon
suddenly made the tide of your body fall.
Like oiled wrestlers at a festival
who feel their adversary slide between their arms

powerless I felt you slip from mine
under the moon's light white as this wine as your teeth
  which made you so gay
as you fluttered wildly in the circle of the dance
while your mother warned you not to come near me.

I looked up at the sky from the depths of my hut;
the moon was only a smile, your white smile congealed.

Cape Verde Islands

Aguinaldo Fonseca

Tavern by the Sea

A distant glimmer
And a beacon spitting light
In the black face of night.

Everything is brine and yearning.

Winds with waves on their back
Make tremble the tavern
Which is an anchored ship.

Love passionate and brutal
Amidst the open knives
And the abandon
Of a prostitute's embrace.

Upon the air despairings rise
In heavy swells of smoke.

Bottles, glasses, bottles . . .
– Oh! the thirst of a sailor . . .

Tattooings pricked on skin
Proclaim the pain and the bravado
Of escapades in ports.

Men of every race,
Men without homeland or name
– Just men of the sea
With voice of salt and wind
And ships in unclouded eyes.

Boredom and longing appear
Chewing on aged pipes . . .
Appear and then depart
Staggering off with a drunk.

Cards, tables, and chairs,
Bottles, glasses, bottles
And the tavern-keeper's face
Stirring up ancient quarrels.

And everything is full of sin
And everything is full of sleep
And everything is full of sea!

São Tomé

Aldo do Espirito Santo

Where are the Men Seized in this Wind of Madness?

Blood falling in drops to the earth
men dying in the forest
and blood falling, falling . . .
on those cast into the sea. . . .
Fernão Dias for ever in the story
of Ilha Verde, red with blood,
of men struck down
in the vast arena of the quay.
Alas the quay, the blood, the men,
the fetters, the lash of beatings
resound, resound, resound
dropping in the silence of prostrated lives
of cries, and howls of pain
from men who are men no more,
in the hands of nameless butchers.
Zé Mulato, in the story of the quay
shooting men in the silence
of bodies falling.
Alas Zé Mulato, Zé Mulato,
The victims cry for vengeance
The sea, the sea of Fernão Dias
devouring human lives
is bloody red.
– We are arisen –
Our eyes are turned to you.
Our lives entombed

in fields of death,
men of the Fifth of February
men fallen in the furnace of death
imploring pity
screaming for life,
dead without air, without water
they all arise
from the common grave
and upright in the chorus of justice
cry for vengeance. . . .
   The fallen bodies in the forest,
the homes, the homes of men
destroyed in the gulf
of ravening fire,
lives incinerated,
raise the unaccustomed chorus of justice
crying for vengeance.
And all you hangmen
all you torturers
sitting in the dock:
– What have you done with my people? . . .
– What do you answer?
– Where is my people? . . .
And I answer in the silence
of voices raised
demanding justice. . . .
One by one, through all the line. . . .
For you, tormentors,
forgiveness has no name.
Justice shall be heard.
And the blood of lives fallen
in the forests of death,
innocent blood
drenching the earth
in a silence of terrors
shall make the earth fruitful,
crying for justice.

It is the flame of humanity
singing of hope
in a world without bonds
where liberty
is the fatherland of men. ....

Angola

Agostinho Neto

Farewell at the Moment of Parting

My mother
(oh black mothers whose children have departed)
you taught me to wait and to hope
as you have done through the disastrous hours

But in me
life has killed that mysterious hope

I wait no more
it is I who am awaited

Hope is ourselves
your children
travelling towards a faith that feeds life

We the naked children of the bush sanzalas
unschooled urchins who play with balls of rags
on the noonday plains
ourselves
hired to burn out our lives in coffee fields
ignorant black men
who must respect the whites
and fear the rich
we are your children of the native quarters
which the electricity never reaches
men dying drunk
abandoned to the rhythm of death's tom-toms
your children
who hunger

who thirst
who are ashamed to call you mother
who are afraid to cross the streets
who are afraid of men

It is ourselves
the hope of life recovered.

African Poem

There on the horizon
the fire
and the dark silhouettes of the imbondeiro trees
with their arms raised
in the air the green smell of burnt palm trees

On the road
the line of Bailundo porters
groaning under their loads of crueira*

in the room
the sweet sweet-eyed mulatress
retouching her face with rouge and rice-powder
the woman under her many clothes moving her hips
on the bed
the sleepless man thinking
of buying knives and forks to eat with at a table

On the sky the reflections
of the fire
and the silhouette of the blacks at the drums
with their arms raised
in the air the warm tune of marimbas

On the road the porters
in the room the mulatress
on the bed the sleepless man

  * Crueira = maize flour.

The burning coals consuming
consuming with fire
the warm country of the horizons.

Kinaxixi

I was glad to sit down
on a bench in Kinaxixi
at six o'clock of a hot evening
and just sit there . . .

Someone would come
maybe
to sit beside me

And I would see the black faces
of the people going uptown
in no hurry
expressing absence in the
jumbled Kimbundu they conversed in.

I would see the tired footsteps
of the servants whose fathers also were servants
looking for love here, glory there, wanting
something more than drunkenness in every
alcohol.

Neither happiness nor hate.

After the sun had set
lights would be turned on and I
would wander off
thinking that our life after all is simple
too simple
for anyone who is tired and still has to walk.

Antonio Jacinto

Monangamba

On that big estate there is no rain
it's the sweat of my brow that waters the crops:

On that big estate there is coffee ripe
and that cherry-redness
is drops of my blood turned sap.

> The coffee will be roasted,
> ground, and crushed,
> will turn black, black with the colour of the
>   *contratado*.*

Black with the colour of the *contratado*!

Ask the birds that sing,
the streams in carefree wandering
and the high wind from inland:

> Who gets up early? Who goes to toil?
> Who is it carries on the long road
> the hammock or bunch of kernels?
> Who reaps and for pay gets scorn
> rotten maize, rotten fish,
> ragged clothes, fifty *angolares*†
> beating for biting back?

Who?

> Who makes the millet grow

* *contratado* =contract labourer.   †*angolares* =unit of money.

and the orange groves to flower?
– Who?

Who gives the money for the boss to buy
cars, machinery, women
and Negro heads for the motors?

Who makes the white man prosper,
grow big-bellied – get much money?
– Who?

And the birds that sing,
the streams in carefree wandering
and the high wind from inland
will answer:

– Monangambeeee. . . .

Ah! Let me at least climb the palm trees
Let me drink wine, palm wine
and fuddled by my drunkness forget

– Monangambeee. . . .

South Africa

Mazisi Kunene

To the Proud

In the twirling mountains overhung with mist
Foretell Nodongo the proud name of the subsequent hours
Since, when you beat the loud music of your wings,
The secret night creeps underneath the measured time.

When you behold the fixed bulk of the sun
Jubilant in its uncertain festivals
Know that the symbol on which you stand shall vanish
Now that the dawning awaits us with her illusions.

Assemble the little hum of your pealing boast
For the sake of the reward meted to Somndeni
Who sat abundantly pride-flowing
Till the passer-by vultures of heaven overtook him.

We who stood by you poverty-stricken
Shall abandon you to the insanity of licence
And follow the winding path
Where the wisdom granaries hold increase.

Then shall your nakedness show
Teasing you before the unashamed sun.
Itching you shall unfurl the night
But we the sons of Time shall be our parents' race.

The Echoes

Over the vast summer hills
I shall commission the maternal sun
To fetch you with her long tilted rays,

The slow heave of the valleys
Will once again roll the hymns of accompaniment
Scattering the glitter of the milky way over the bare fields.

You will meet me
Underneath the shadow of the timeless earth
Where I lie weaving the seasons.

You will indulge in the sway dances of your kin
To the time of symphonic flutes
Ravishing the identity of water lilies.

I have opened the mountain gates
So that the imposing rim
Of the Ruwenzori shall steal your image.

Even the bubbling lips of continents
(To the shy palms of Libya)
Shall awake the long-forgotten age.

The quivering waters of the Zambezi river
Will bear on a silvery blanket your name
Leading it to the echoing of the sea.

Let me not love you alone
Lest the essence of your being
Lie heavy on my tongue
When you count so many to praise.

Farewell

O beloved farewell. . . .
Hold these leaping dreams of fire
With the skeletal hands of death
So that when hungry night encroaches
You defy her stubborn intrigues.

Do not look to where we turn and seethe
We pale humanity, like worms
(The ululations might bind you to our grief)
Whose feet carry the duty of life.

Farewell beloved
Even the hush that haunts the afternoon
Will sing the ding-dong drum of your ultimate joy
Where we sit by the fireside tossing the memories
Making the parts fit into each day complete;
Yet knowing ours is a return of emptiness

Farewell, yewu . . . ye.

As Long as I Live

When I still can remember
When I still have eyes to see
When I still have hands to hold
When I still have feet to drag
So long shall I bear your name with all the days
So long shall I stare at you with all the stars of heaven
Though you lead me to their sadistic beasts
I shall find a way to give my burden-love
Blaming your careless truths on yesterdays.
Because I swear by life herself
When you still live, so shall I live
Turning the night into day, forcing her
To make you lie pompous on its pathways.

So shall I wander around the rim of the sun
Till her being attains your fullness
As long as I live. . . .

Elegy

O Mzingeli son of the illustrious clans
You whose beauty spreads across the Tukela estuary
Your memory haunts like two eagles
We have come to the ceremonial ruins
We come to mourn the bleeding sun
We are the children of Ndungunya of the Dlamini clan
They whose grief strikes fear over the earth
We carry the long mirrors in the afternoon
Recasting time's play past infinite night.

O great departed ancestors
You promised us immortal life with immortal joys
But how you deceived us!

We invited the ugly salamander
To keep watch over a thousand years with a thousand
    sorrows
She watched to the far end of the sky
Sometimes terrorized by the feet of departed men
One day the furious storms
One day from the dark cyclone
One day in the afternoon
We gazed into a barren desert
Listening to the tremendous voices in the horizon
And loved again in the epics
And loved incestuous love!

We count a million
Strewn in the dust of ruined capitals
The bull tramples us on an anthill

We are late in our birth
Accumulating violent voices
Made from the lion's death
You whose love comes from the stars
Have mercy on us!
Give us the crown of thunder
That our grief may overhang the earth

O we are naked at the great streams
Wanderers greet us no more. . . .

Bloke Modisane

lonely

it gets awfully lonely,
lonely;
like screaming,
screaming lonely;
screaming down dream alley,
screaming of blues, like none can hear;
but you hear me clear and loud:
echoing loud;
like it's for you I scream.

I talk to myself when I write,
shout and scream to myself,
then to myself
scream and shout:
shouting a prayer,
screaming noises,
knowing this way I tell
the world about still lives;
even maybe
just to scream and shout.

is it I lack the musician's contact
direct?
or, is it true, the writer
creates
(except the trinity with God, the machine and he)

incestuous silhouettes
to each other scream and shout,
to me shout and scream
pry and mate;
inbred deformities of loneliness.

Dennis Brutus

At a Funeral

Black, green and gold at sunset: pageantry
And stubbled graves Expectant, of eternity,
In bride's-white, nun's-white veils the nurses gush their
    bounty.
Of red-wine cloaks, frothing the bugled dirging slopes
Salute! Then ponder all this hollow panoply
For one whose gifts the mud devours, with our hopes.

Oh all you frustrate ones, powers tombed in dirt,
Aborted, not by Death but carrion books of birth
Arise! The brassy shout of Freedom stirs our earth;
Not death but death's-head tyranny scythes our ground
And plots our narrow cells of pain defeat and dearth:
Better that we should die, than that we should lie down.

*(For Valencia Majombosi, who died shortly after qualifying as
a doctor.)*

Nightsong City

Sleep well, my love, sleep well:
the harbour lights glaze over restless docks,
police cars cockroach through the tunnel streets;

from the shanties creaking iron-sheets
violence like a bug-infested rag is tossed
and fear is immanent as sound in the wind-swung bell;

the day's long anger pants from sand and rocks;
but for this breathing night at least,
my land, my love, sleep well.

Gaily Teetering

Gaily teetering on the bath's edge
one long bare arm outflung to balance
the sweep of satin flanks and thews,
face-level the brown triangular fuzz
grey glistening with a hoar of drops,
'Kiss me!' you cried, and 'No!' morosely I.

Etched aloft against the prison-grey light
that filtered through the plastic curtaining
the smooth flesh surging tautly over
the thoracic cage to where the nipples gazed
in blandly unselfconscious innocence,
'Kiss me!' you cried, and 'No!' morosely I,

seeing within the cage the soon too-tired muscle
and all this animal spirit spent,
this emphasis on sheer carnality
reiteration of mortality
and all immediate joys ephemeral,
angered and wounded, 'No!' and 'No!' I cried.

This Sun on this Rubble

This sun on this rubble after rain.
Bruised though we must be
some easement we require
unarguably, though we argue against desire.
Under jackboots our bones and spirits crunch

forced into sweat-tear-sodden slush
– now glow-lipped by this sudden touch:

– sun-stripped perhaps, our bones may later sing
or spell out some malignant nemesis
Sharpevilled to spearpoints for revenging
but now our pride-dumbed mouths are wide
in wordless supplication
– are grateful for the least relief from pain
– like this sun on this debris after rain.

William Kgositsile

The Air I Hear

The air, I hear,
froze to the sound
searching. And my memory
present and future tickles
the womb like the pulse
of this naked air
in the eye of a tear
drop. The dead cannot
remember even the memory
of death's laughter. But memory
defiant like the sound of pain
rides the wave at dawn
in the marrow of the desert
palm: stands looking still
and the bitter shape
of yesterdays weaves
timeless tomorrows
in the leaves
of laughter larger than
singular birth . . .

K. A. Nortje

Up Late

Night here, the owners asleep upstairs:
the room's eyes shut, its voices dead,
though I admire it when its mirrors
oblige me with my presence. Looking ahead
needs glancing back to what I once
was, the time that mischance
borrowed my body to break it by terror.

Now the cameras rest in their elegant
leather coffins, having caught
the whirl of streets before the wheels go silent.
Rain trickles as the red biro writes my heart:
time demands no attention of the will,
the clock is yellow with black numerals.
The icebox resumes its purring descant.

This picture opens on the past. I rise
to study a calendar scene from what was home:
an old white mill, sentimental, South African Airways
(the blue lithe buck), peaceful, implausible. Some
fugitive sense holds back the bruising wave:
that gift to spend, my song where I arrive,
didn't I take it from the first dispiriting wilderness?

My mind burned and I shackled it
with squalid love, the violence of the flesh.
The quiet scars over my veins bit
less deep now than the knife or lash

could feel content about:
no longer need I shout
freedom in the house. I sit in light

here, the refugee's privilege. Nor do I want
fruit in a bowl, banana pleasure, the skin
that slides from my fingers, spent
because the soft heart only must be eaten.
Give me the whole experience to savour
who have known waste and also favour:
time to come may find me eloquent

in other rooms, that reminisce
of this one so composed in silence. Love,
the necessary pain, has spurred a search.
Moving from place to place I always have
come some way closer to knowing
the final sequence of song that's going
to master the solitudes night can teach.

At Rest From the Grim Place

The sergeant laughs with strong teeth,
his jackboots nestle under the springbok horns.
Those bayonets are silent,
the spear of the nation gone to the ground.
Warriors prowl in the stars of their dungeons.
I've seen the nebulae of a man's eyes
squirm with pain, he sang his life
through cosmic volleys. They call it
genital therapy, the blond bosses.

Why is there no more news?
Bluetits scuffle in the eaves of England,
an easy summer shimmers on the water.
Fields of peace, I lie here
in the music of your gaze

so beautiful we seem no strangers.
Curling smoke, a white butt is
brother to my lips and fingers.
You watch the ash on grass blades gently crumble.
Your hands are small as roses,
they cancel memory.

Once going down to the sea through the mountains
my limbs felt freedom in the glide of air:
over the bridge at the window I found
speech an impossible cry.
Under the fatal shadows spun down the chasm
my heart squirmed in the throat of snaking water.
I have since forgotten what they call that place.

Malawi

David Rubadiri

An African Thunderstorm

From the west
Clouds come hurrying with the wind
Turning
Sharply
Here and there
Like a plague of locusts
Whirling
Tossing up things on its tail
Like a madman chasing nothing.

Pregnant clouds
Ride stately on its back
Gathering to perch on hills
Like dark sinister wings;
The Wind whistles by
And trees bend to let it pass.

In the village
Screams of delighted children
Toss and turn
In the din of whirling wind,
Women –
Babies clinging on their backs –
Dart about
In and out
Madly
The Wind whistles by
Whilst trees bend to let it pass.

MALAWI

Clothes wave like tattered flags
Flying off
To expose dangling breasts
As jaggered blinding flashes
Rumble, tremble, and crack
Amidst the smell of fired smoke
And the pelting march of the storm.

Kenya

John Mbiti

New York Skyscrapers

The weak scattered rays of yellow sun
Peeped through the hazy tissues
That blanketed them with transparent wax;
And as the wrinkled rays closed the day,
Smoky chimneys of New York coughed
Looking down in bended towers
And vomited sad tears of dark smoke.

Joseph Kariuki

Come Away, my Love

Come away, my love, from streets
Where unkind eyes divide,
And shop windows reflect our difference.
In the shelter of my faithful room rest.

There, safe from opinions, being behind
Myself, I can see only you;
And in my dark eyes your grey
Will dissolve.
         The candlelight throws
Two dark shadows on the wall
Which merge into one as I close beside you.

When at last the lights are out,
And I feel your hand in mine,
Two human breaths join in one,
And the piano weaves
Its unchallenged harmony.

Khadambi Asalache

Death of a Chief

pavements lined
sorrowful silence
tears
the coffin off to somewhere
in black
behind it the entire district
involved
in songs of grief
that flow and follow
a trailing gesture
thoughts
battered syllables
on lips

as past periods
return
in the farewell
of the blank faces
to float a fable
dreams
years of his reign

the path is silent
to this procession
walking into a myth
as he passes
alone
freed from praises

the worldly notion
the sensate achievement that floats
on tongues like a wind
like changeable news

this slow walk seems
a readjustment
from his life
a transit
a sampling of the fragrance
of death and the surprise of
its calm
an eternal grip
cold

Uganda

Okot p'Bitek

from *The Song of Lawino*

Listen, my clansmen,
I cry over my husband
Whose head is lost.
Ocol has lost his head
In the forest of books.

When my husband
Was still wooing me
His eyes were still alive,
His ears were still unblocked,
Ocol had not yet become a fool
My friend was a man then!

He had not yet become a woman,
He was still a free man,
His heart was still his chief.

My husband was still a Black man
The son of the Bull
The son of Agik
The woman from Okol
Was still a man,
An Acoli. . . .

The papers on my husband's desk
Coil threateningly
Like the giant forest climbers,
Like the kituba tree

That squeezes other trees to death;
Some stand up,
Others lie on their backs,
They are inter-locked
Like the legs of youths
At the orak dance,
Like the legs of the planks
Of the goggo fence,
They are tightly interlocked
Like the legs of the giant forest climbers
In the impenetrable forest.

My husband's house
Is a mighty forest of books,
Dark it is and very damp,
The steam rising from the ground
Hot thick and poisonous
Mingles with the corrosive dew
And the rain drops
That have collected in the leaves. . . .
O, my clansmen,

Let us all cry together!
Come,
Let us mourn the death of my husband,
The death of a Prince
The Ash that was produced
By a great Fire!
O, this homestead is utterly dead,
Close the gates
With lacari thorns,
For the Prince
The heir to the Stool is lost!
And all the young men
Have perished in the wilderness!
And the fame of this homestead
That once blazed like a wild fire
In a moonless night

Is now like the last breaths
Of a dying old man!

There is not one single true son left,
The entire village
Has fallen into the hands
Of war captives and slaves!
Perhaps one of our boys
Escaped with his life!
Perhaps he is hiding in the bush
Waiting for the sun to set!

But will he come?
Before the next mourning?
Will he arrive in time?

Bile burns my inside!
I feel like vomiting!
For all our young men
Were finished in the forest,
Their manhood was finished
In the class-rooms,
Their testicles
Were smashed
With large books!

Moçambique

José Craveirinha

The Seed is in Me

Dead or living
the seed is in me
in the universal whiteness of my bones

All feel
uneasiness
at the undoubted whiteness of my bones
white as the breasts of Ingrids or Marias
in Scandinavian lands
or in Polana the smart quarter
of my old native town.

All feel
uneasiness
that the mingling in my veins should be
blood from the blood of every blood
and instead of the peace ineffable of pure and simple birth
and a pure and simple death
breed a rash of complexes
from the seed of my bones.

But a night with the massaleiras heavy with green fruit
batuques swirl above the sweating stones
and the tears of rivers

All feel
uneasiness
at the white seed in me
breeding a rash inflamed with malediction.

And one day
will come all the Marias of the distant nations
penitent or no
weeping
laughing
or loving to the rhythm of a song

To say to my bones
forgive us, brother.

Three Dimensions

In the cabin . . .
the god of the machine
in cap and overalls
holds in his hand the secret of the pistons.

In the carriage . . .
the first-class god
elaborates his schemes in regulated air.

And on the branch-line . . .
– feet flat against the steel of the coaches –
bursting his lungs
the god of the trolley.

Noemia de Sousa

Appeal

Who has strangled the tired voice
of my forest sister?
On a sudden, her call to action
was lost in the endless flow of night and day.
No more it reaches me every morning,
wearied with long journeying,
mile after mile drowned
in the everlasting cry: Macala!

No, it comes no more, still damp with dew,
leashed with children and submission. . . .
One child on her back, another in her womb
– always, always, always!
And a face all compassed in a gentle look,
whenever I recall that look I feel
my flesh and blood swell tremulous,
throbbing to revelations and affinities. . . .
– But who has stopped her immeasurable look
from feeding my deep hunger after comradeship
that my poor table never will serve to satisfy?

Io mamane, who can have shot the noble voice
of my forest sister?
What mean and brutal rhino-whip
has lashed until it killed her?

– In my garden the seringa blooms.
But with an evil omen in its purple flower,

in its intense inhuman scent;
and the wrap of tenderness spread by the sun
over the light mat of petals
has waited since summer for my sister's child
to rest himself upon it. . . .
In vain, in vain,
a chirico sings and sings perched among the garden reeds,
for the little boy of my missing sister,
the victim of the forest's vaporous dawns.
Ah, I know, I know: at the last there was a glitter
of farewell in those gentle eyes,
and her voice came like a murmur hoarse,
tragic and despairing. . . .

O Africa, my motherland, answer me:
What was done to my forest sister,
that she comes no more to the city with her eternal little
    ones
(one on her back, one in her womb),
with her eternal charcoal-vendor's cry?
O Africa, my motherland,
you at least will not forsake my heroic sister,
she shall live in the proud memorial of your arms!

Valente Malangatana

To the Anxious Mother

Into your arms I came
when you bore me, very anxious
you, who were so alarmed
at that monstrous moment
fearing that God might take me.
Everyone watched in silence
to see if the birth was going well
everyone washed their hands
to be able to receive the one who came from Heaven
and all the women were still and afraid.
But when I emerged
from the place where you sheltered me so long
at once I drew my first breath
at once you cried out with joy
the first kiss was my grandmother's.
And she took me at once to the place
where they kept me, hidden away
everyone was forbidden to enter my room
because everyone smelt bad
and I all fresh, fresh
breathed gently, wrapped in my napkins.
But grandmother, who seemed like a madwoman,
always looking and looking again
because the flies came at me
and the mosquitoes harried me
God who also watched over me
was my old granny's friend.

Woman

In the cool waters of the river
we shall have fish that are huge
which shall give the sign of
the end of the world perhaps
because they will make an end of woman
woman who adorns the fields
woman who is the fruit of man.

The flying fish makes an end of searching
because woman is the gold of man
when she sings she ever seems
like the fado-singer's well-tuned guitar
when she dies, I shall cut off
her hair to deliver me from sin.

Woman's hair shall be the blanket
over my coffin when another Artist
calls me to Heaven to paint me
woman's breasts shall be my pillow
woman's eye shall open up for me the way to heaven
woman's belly shall give birth to me up there
and woman's glance shall watch me
as I go up to Heaven.

Sources of the Poems

Sources of the Poems

AIG-IMOUKHUEDE: poem from MS.

APRONTI: poem from *Transition*.

ASALACHE: poem from MS.

AWOONOR-WILLIAMS: 'Lovers' Song', 'Weaver Bird' and 'Easter Dawn' from *Rediscovery*, Mbari, Ibadan, 1964. Other poems from *Okyeame*, 1 (1961).

BOGNINI: both poems from *Ce dur appel de l'espoir*, Présence Africaine, 1960.

BOLAMBA: all poems from *Esanzo*.

BOUNDZEKI-DONGALA: poem from *Nouvelle Somme*.

BREW: both poems from *Okyeame*, 1 (1961).

BRUTUS: poems from *Sirens Knuckles Boots*, Mbari, Ibadan, 1963.

CLARK: 'A Child Asleep', 'The Leader' and 'His Excellency the Masquerader' from *A Reed in the Tide*, Longmans, 1965. Other poems from Mbari Publications, Ibadan, 1962.

CRAVEIRINHA: both poems from Andrade's anthology.

DE SOUSA: poem from Andrade's anthology.

DIOP (BIRAGO): all poems from *Leurres et lueurs*.

DIOP (DAVID): all poems from *Coups de pilon*.

DIPOKO: 'Pain' and revised version of 'Exile' from MS., 'Our Life' from *Transition*.

ECHERUO: 'Melting Pot' and 'Easter Penitence' from *Black Orpheus*, 'Sophia' from MS.

EGUDU: poem from *Black Orpheus*.

FONSECA: poem from Andrade's anthology.

HIGO: both poems from *Transition*.

JACINTO: poem from Andrade's anthology.

KARIUKI: poem from MS.

KAYO: poem from *Nouvelle Somme*.

KGOSITSILE: poem from *Transition*.

KOMEY: poem from *Black Orpheus*.

KUNENE: all poems from MS.

MALANGATANA: both poems from *Black Orpheus*.

MBITI: poem from MS.

MODISANE: poem from MS.

NDU: poem from *Black Orpheus*.

NETO: 'African Poem' and 'Kinaxixi' from *Black Orpheus*, translated by W. S. Merwin, 'Farewell at the Moment of Parting' from Andrade's anthology.

NOKAN: poem from *Nouvelle Somme*.

NORTJE: both poems from MS.

OKARA: 'The Snowflakes Sail Gently Down' and 'The Mystic Drum' from *Reflections*, 'Adhiambo' and 'One Night at Victoria Beach' from MSS. 'Were I to Choose', 'Piano and Drums' and 'Spirit of the Wind' from *Black Orpheus*.

OKIGBO: 'Water Maid', 'Bridge', 'Suddenly becoming talkative', 'For he was a shrub among the poplars', 'Banks of reed' and two sections of 'Distances' from *Transition*; other poems from *Heavensgate*, Mbari Publications, Ibadan, 1963.

OLOGOUDOU: both poems from *Nouvelle Somme*.

P'BITEK, OKOT: from *The Song of Lawin*, Nairobi, 1966.

PETERS: 'Parachute Men', 'One Long Jump' and 'She Came in Silken Drapes' from *Poems*, Mbari, Ibadan, 1964; other poems from *Black Orpheus*.

RABÉARIVELO: all poems from Senghor's anthology. English versions from *24 Poems*, Mbari Publications, Ibadan, 1963.

RANAIVO: both poems from Senghor's anthology.

RUBADIRI: poem from MS.

SANTO: poem from Andrade's anthology.

SENGHOR: 'In Memoriam', 'Night of Sine', 'Luxembourg 1939', 'Totem', 'Paris in the Snow', 'Blues', 'The Dead', 'Prayer to Masks', 'Visit' and 'All Day Long' from *Chants d'ombres* and *Hosties noires*, 'In what Tempestuous Night' and 'New York' from *Ethiopiques*, 'You Held the Black Face', 'I will Pronounce your Name' and 'Be not Amazed' from *Chants pour Naëtt*.

SOYINKA: 'Season' from *Encounter*, 'Telephone Conversation' from *Ibadan*, 'Death in the Dawn' from *Black Orpheus*, and 'Prisoner' from *Reflections*, A.U.P., Lagos, 1962; 'Massacre, October 1966' and 'Civilian and Soldier' from *Idanre*, Methuen, 1967; other poems from MSS.

TATI: both poems from MS.

U TAM'SI: all poems from *Feu de Brousse* and *Epitomé*.

WONODI: 'Planting' from *Ucheke*, Mbari, Ibadan, 1964, 'Salute to Icheke' from *Black Orpheus*.

YAMBO: poem from *Nouvelle Somme*.

The following key works are referred to above and in the following Notes:

Senghor's anthology: *Nouvelle Anthologie de la poésie nègre et malgache*, edited by L. S. Senghor, with an introduction, *L'Orphée noir*, by Jean-Paul Sartre (Paris, Presses Universitaires de France, 1948).

Andrade's *Caderno*: *Caderno da poesia negra de expressão portuguesa* edited by Mario de Andrade (Lisbon, 1953).

Andrade's anthology: *Antologia da poesia negra de expressão portuguesa* by Mario de Andrade and preceded by *Cultura negro-africana e assimilacão* (Paris, Oswald, 1958).

Black Orpheus: Journal of African and Afro-American Literature, published twice or thrice yearly 1957–63, from the Ministry of Education, Ibadan, Nigeria; since 1963, published for the Mbari Club, Ibadan, by Longmans.

Nouvelle Somme: 'Nouvelle Somme de Poésie du Monde Noir', Présence Africaine No. 57, 1966.

Présence Africaine: Cultural Review of the Negro World, published regularly since 1947, of recent years bi-monthly and in both French and English editions, by Présence Africaine, Paris.

Transition: published bi-monthly in Kampala since 1961.

Notes on the Authors

Notes on the Authors

AIG-IMOUKHUEDE, FRANK: b. 1935 at Edunabon, near Ife in the Yoruba country of Western Nigeria, though his home is in Benin Province. Attended at least fifteen primary schools, then Ibgobi College and University College, Ibadan, where he contributed poetry to J. P. Clark's *The Horn*. Recently worked for a national daily in Lagos and is now back in Ibadan as an Information Officer. Has written a number of plays for broadcasting. The first of the young Nigerian poets to attempt writing in pidgin English. Two of his poems have appeared in *Black Orpheus*.

APRONTI, JAWA: b. 1940 in Ghana, read English at University of Ghana and later studied Linguistics at Leeds. First published poetry in *Transition*.

ASALACHE, KHADAMBI: b. 1934 at Kaimosi, Kenya. After studies in architecture and art at Nairobi and Vienna, went to London 1959 and has worked at variety of jobs, including TV script-writing. His first novel, *A Calabash of Life*, has been published by Longmans.

AWOONOR-WILLIAMS, GEORGE: b. 1935 at Wheta, near Keta in the Togo Region of Ghana, of Sierra Leonian and Togolese descent. Educated at Achimota and the University of Ghana, where he later worked in the Institute of African Studies, specializing in vernacular poetry. Edits the Ghanaian literary review *Okeyeame*, in which some of his poems have appeared. His first volume of poems *Rediscovery*, was published by Mbari in 1964.

BOGNINI, JOSEPH MIEZAN: b. 1936 at Grand Bassam, Ivory Coast. Went to Paris 1958 to study architecture. First book of poems, *Ce dur appel de l'espoir*, published by Présence Africaine in 1960.

BOLAMBA, ANTOINE-ROGER: born in the former Belgian Congo. Has published numerous articles and poems in the review *La Voix du Congolais*, of which he was editor. Influenced by Césaire. Has published *Esanzo*, poems (Présence Africaine, 1956).

BOUNDZEKI-DONGALA, EMMANUEL: No information.

BREW, KWESI: b. 1928 at Cape Coast in Ghana. Graduated at the University of Ghana. Published poetry in the first number of the Ghanaian literary review *Okyeame*. Now working at the Foreign Office at Accra.

BRUTUS, DENNIS: b. Rhodesia and taught for ten years at Government High School in Port Elizabeth. Dismissed in 1961 and banned from all gatherings. Went to Witwatersrand University on scholarship to read law. A keen sportsman, was arrested by Portuguese police whilst attempting to leave Swaziland to attend the International Olympic Committee at Baden. Shot and wounded by South African police in Johannesburg and jailed for eighteen months. Went to England to live in 1966. First book of poems, *Sirens Knuckles Boots*, published by Mbari, 1963.

CLARK, JOHN PEPPER: b. 1935 in the Ijaw country of the Niger Delta, Nigeria. Educated at Government College, Warri, and the University College, Ibadan. While at Ibadan founded an influential poetry magazine, *The Horn*. From 1960 worked as a journalist in Ibadan and Lagos and then went to Princeton on a fellowship. He has published several poems in *Black Orpheus* and his first play, *Song of a Goat*, was produced at Ibadan and Enugu in 1962. A free spirit and an abundant talent. Has published *Song of a Goat*, (Mbari, Ibadan, 1962) and *Poems* (Mbari, 1962), *America, their America* (André Deutsch, 1964), *A Reed in the Tide*, poems (Longmans, 1965), *Three Plays* (O.U.P., 1964), and *Ozidi*, play (O.U.P., 1966).

CRAVEIRINHA, JOSÉ: b. 1922 at Lourenço Marques, where he works as a journalist. His poems have appeared in various periodicals and in Andrade's anthology.

DE SOUSA, NOEMIA: b. 1927 at Lourenço Marques. The first African woman to achieve a genuine reputation as a modern poet, she has published poetry in a number of Brazilian, Angolan and Moçambique journals and in Andrade's *Caderno* and anthology.

DIOP, BIRAGO: b. 1906 at Dakar, Senegal. Studied at Lycée Faidherbe in St Louis and later qualified as a veterinary surgeon. Has spent much of his life in Upper Volta as a government veterinary officer. His output is small, but carefully and exquisitely composed. Had several poems in Senghor's anthology. Has published *Leurres et lueurs*, poems (Présence Africaine, 1960), *Les Contes d'Amadou Koumba* (Paris, Fasquelle, 1947), *Les Nouveaux Contes d'Amadou Koumba* (Présence Africaine, 1958).

DIOP, DAVID: b. 1927 at Bordeaux of a Senegalese father and a Cameroonian mother. Killed in an air-crash off Dakar in 1960. Throughout his short life Diop was in poor health and was often in hospital. Moved frequently from his childhood onwards between France and West Africa. Was a regular contributor to *Présence Africaine* and had several early poems in Senghor's anthology. Has published *Coups de pilon*, poems (Présence Africaine, 1956).

DIPOKO, MBELLA SONNE: b. 1936 at Mungo, near Duala, Cameroons. Educated in West Cameroon and Nigeria. Joined news staff of Radio Nigeria 1957 and left 1960 whilst on Paris assignment. Since then has lived in Paris and devoted himself mainly to writing. Poems have appeared in various journals; a novel, *A Few Nights and Days*, the first of a trilogy, was published by Longmans in 1966.

ECHERUO, MICHAEL: b. 1937 in Owerri Province in the Ibo country of Eastern Nigeria. Educated at Stella Maris College, Port Harcourt, and University College, Ibadan, where he read English. Now lecturing in English at the University of Nsukka. He produced J. P. Clark's *Song of a Goat* at Enugu in 1962. His poems were first published in *Black Orpheus*, No. 12.

EGUDU, ROMANUS: b. Eastern Nigeria and educated at Nsukka University, where he is now Lecturer in English and African Literature. Wrote his post-graduate thesis in America on Ibo Traditional Poetry. Has published poetry in *Black Orpheus*.

FONSECA, AGUINALDO: b. 1922 in the Cape Verde Islands. Has worked on numerous literary reviews, including *Seara Nova*, *Atlantico*, and *Nundo Literario* and has contributed to Andrade's anthology. Has published *Linha do horizonte*, poems (Edição da Seccão de Cabo Verde da Casa dos Estudantes do Império, Lisbon, 1951).

HIGO, AIG: b. Nigeria. Read English at Ibadan University and did post-graduate work at Leeds. Now works as publisher's representative in Nigeria.

JACINTO, ANTONIO: born in Luanda, Angola. His poems have appeared in Andrade's *Caderno* and anthology.

KARIUKI, JOSEPH: b. 1929 in the Kikuyu country of Kenya. Educated at Makerere College in Uganda and taught for several years in Kenya before coming to England to read English at King's College, Cambridge. An occasional broadcaster while in England, he returned to Kenya in 1962 and is now Principal of the Institute of Public Administration.

KAYO, PATRICE: teaches at Bafoussam, Cameroons.

KGOSITSILE, WILLIAM: b. 1938 in Johannesburg. Left South Africa and worked for a while for *Spearhead* magazine in Dar es Salaam. Has been studying in various American Universities since 1962.

KOMEY, ELLIS AYITEY: b. 1927 at Accra. Educated at Accra Academy. Has published poetry in *Black Orpheus* and *West African Review*. Later African Editor of *Flamingo*.

KUNENE, MAZISI: b. 1930 in Durban, where he took his M.A. at Natal University. Came to London in 1959 to work on a thesis on Zulu poetry. Now engaged on political work and writing an epic concerning the origin and purpose of life as understood in Zulu tradition. Has written a number of vernacular poems and plays, some of which have been published in South Africa. Won the Bantu Literary Competition in 1956.

MALANGATANA, VALENTE: b. 1936 at Marraçuene in Moçambique. Began drawing as a boy. During his childhood his mother unexpectedly went mad, and his father was frequently away at the mines in South Africa. While working as a servant at the Lourenço Marques Club he attended night school and began painting 'furiously'. He was discovered painting one night by the brilliant architect Amançio Guedes, who took him into his studio. Since then he has worked both as a decorative artist on architectural schemes and as a painter of great force and originality. In addition to a number of poems, he has completed an autobiography. Some of his poetry has appeared in *Black Orpheus* together with an account of his painting.

MBITI, JOHN: b. 1931 at Kitui in the Kamba country of Kenya. Educated at Alliance High School, Makerere College, and Barrington College, U.S.A., where he was ordained. Later took a doctorate at Westminster College, Cambridge. Has published several books in Kikamba, his mother tongue, and has contributed poems and stories to various periodicals in Europe. Is now teaching Religious Studies at Makerere University College in Uganda.

MODISANE, BLOKE: b. 1923 at Johannesburg, where he was educated. Worked for some years on *Drum* magazine but fled from South Africa a few years ago and now lives and works in London as a writer, actor, and broadcaster. Has published short stories and articles in many periodicals. He played a leading role in the London production of Genet's *The Blacks*. His autobiography, *Blame Me on History* was published by Thames & Hudson in 1964. Recently spent a year on historical research in Africa and Germany, preparing a book on the Maji Maji Rebellion.

NDU, POL N: b. Eastern Nigeria and studied at Nsukka University, where he now lectures. Poetry first published in *Black Orpheus*.

NETO, AGOSTINHO: b. 1922 at Icola e Bengo in Angola. Studied medicine in Lisbon and returned to practise in Angola. Associated with the movement led by Viriato da Cruz for the 'rediscovery' of Angola's indigenous culture. In 1960 Neto was elected President of the Angolan Liberation Movement, M.P.L.A. In 1960 he was arrested and taken to Portugal for imprisonment. But in 1962 it was announced that he had escaped from Portugal with the aid of the democratic resistance movement. Has published poetry in Portuguese and Angolan reviews and in Andrade's *Caderno* and anthology.

NOKAN, CHARLES: b. 1937 at Yamoussokro, Ivory Coast.

NORTJE, K. A.: b. 1942 in Cape Province, South Africa. Attended government college for Coloureds till 1964 and taught in high school till 1965, when he went to Jesus College, Oxford, to read English. First published in *Black*

Orpheus at the age of nineteen and won an Mbari Poetry Prize.

OKARA, GABRIEL: b. 1921 in the Ijaw country of the Niger Delta, Nigeria. Educated at Government College, Umuahia, he then became a book-binder. At that time he began to write plays and features for broadcasting. He is now Information Officer with the Eastern Regional Government at Enugu. Several of his poems have appeared in *Black Orpheus*, starting with the first number in 1957. His novel, *The Voice*, was published by André Deutsch (1964). A self-sufficient, deeply read, and thoughtful poet.

OKIGBO, CHRISTOPHER: b. 1932 at Ojoto near Onitsha in the Ibo country of Eastern Nigeria. The imagery of his poetry is often rooted in the groves, shrines and sacred streams of his birthplace. Educated at Government College, Umuahia, and University College, Ibadan, where he read Classics. From 1956 to 1958 he was Private Secretary to the Federal Minister of Research and Information, then taught for two years at Fiditi near Ibadan before joining the Library staff at the University of Nigeria. He was then West African representative of the Cambridge University Press. A voracious reader, whose passion for classical poetry seems to be reflected in his own fastidious craftsmanship. He has published *Heavensgate*, poems (Ibadan, Mbari, 1962), *Limits* (Mbari, 1964). He was killed in action with the Biafran Army in 1967.

OLOGOUDOU, EMILE: b. 1935 in Ouidah. Studied Law and Sociology at the University of Dakar from 1957 to 1960, and Economics and Sociology at the University of Cologne in Federal Germany from 1960 to 1966.

P'BITEK, OKOT: b. 1931 in Gulu, Northern Uganda. Educated at Gulu High School and King's College, Budo, where he wrote and produced an opera. Whilst teaching near Gulu, he played football for Uganda and completed a novel in Lwo, *Lak Tar Miyo Kinyero Wi Lobo* (1953). Later he studied Law at Aberystwyth and Social Anthropology at Oxford, where his B.Litt thesis on traditional songs of the Acoli and Lango was presented in 1963. *The Song of Lawino* was first written in Lwo, and was published in an English version in 1966.

PETERS, LENRIE: b. 1932 at Bathurst. Educated at Bathurst,

Freetown, and Trinity College, Cambridge, where he took a medical degree in 1959. Now practises as a surgeon. He is an amateur singer and broadcaster, and his first novel, *The Second Round*, was published in 1964 by Heinemann. His first volume of poems was published by Mbari, Ibadan, 1964 and his second, Satellites, by Heinemann in 1967.

RABÉARIVELO, JEAN-JOSEPH: b. 1901 at Antananarivo, Madagascar, of a noble but poor family. Left school at thirteen and began writing poetry. His early work is imitative, for he had to teach himself a mastery of French literary form before he could develop his own ardent style. He founded a literary review and led the way in the creation of a new Madagascan literature written in French. Passionate and restless in temperament, he married young and drifted from one job to another. He became a drug-addict and killed himself in 1937 in a mood of despair brought on partly by the persistent refusal of the local officials to let him visit France, the ambition of his life. Several of his poems appeared in Senghor's anthology. Has published *La Coupe de cendres* (1924), *Sylves* (1927), *Volumes* (1928), *Vientes de la Mañana* (Rio de Janeiro), *Presque-songes* (Tananarive, presented by Robert Boudry, chez Henri Vidalie, 1934). An English translation of some of his work, *24 Poems*, was published by Mbari in 1963.

RANAIVO, FLAVIEN: b. 1914 in the Imerina country near Antananarivo, his father being Governor of Arivonimamo. He did not go to school until he was eight and learnt music long before he learnt the alphabet. Since early childhood he has spent much time wandering through the countryside around the capital, and his poetic style is much influenced by vernacular song and ballad forms, especially that called *hain-teny*. Hence his crisp use of language, more authentically Madagascan than Rabéarivelo's. Several of his poems appeared in Senghor's anthology. Has published *L'Ombre et le vent* (Preface by O. Monnoni and Illustrations by Andriamampianina, Tananarive, 1947) and *Mes chansons de toujours* (Paris, 1955).

RUBADIRI, DAVID: b. 1930 in Nyasaland. Educated at Makerere College in Uganda and at King's College, Cambridge, where he took the English Tripos. During the Nyasaland crisis in 1959 he was arrested but went to Cambridge after his release from detention. An active broadcaster while in England, he later returned to Nyasaland to teach. Was Ambassador for Malawi in Washington and New York until 1965, when he joined the staff at Makerere University College.

SANTO, ALDO DO ESPIRITO: b. 1926 in São Tomé, where he works as a teacher. Has published poetry in several reviews of São Tomé and Portugal and in Andrade's *Caderno* and anthology.

SENGHOR, LÉOPOLD SÉDAR: b. 1906 at Joal, an old Portuguese coastal settlement in Senegal. He is of the Serere tribe. His father was a groundnut merchant and a Catholic in a land predominantly Moslem. Senghor passed brilliantly from the local *lycée* and at the age of twenty-two went to the Lycée Louis le Grand in Paris. Later he completed his *agrégation* at the Sorbonne, the first West African to do so. In Paris he met Césaire, Damas and other black poets and intellectuals from the Caribbean area. Prominent as an intellectual and political leader of West Africa for many years, he has been at various times a teacher at the École Nationale de la France d'Outremer, a member of the Council of Europe, a Deputy for Senegal in the French National Assembly, and a minister in the French Government. In 1960 installed as first President of the Independent Republic of Senegal. Senghor is the principal African advocate of Négritude and the first African poet to produce a substantial body of work. His style emerged fully formed in his first book, which contains some of his best poems. These display already his characteristic music and imagery, an imagery of the night and the moon, of tenderness and protective presences. Has published *Chants d'ombres*, poems (Paris, Éditions du Seuil, 1945), *Hosties noires*, poems (Éditions du Seuil, 1948: reissued with *Chants d'ombre*, 1956), *Chants pour Naëtt*, poems (Paris, Seghers, 1949), *Ethiopiques*, poems (Seuil, 1956), *Nocturnes*, poems (Seuil, 1961), *Language et poésie négro-africaine* (published in *Poésie et language*, Maison du Poète, Brussels, 1954), *L'Apport de la poésie négre* (in *Témoignages sur la poésie du demi-siècle*, Maison du Poète, Brussels, 1953), *Esthétique négro-africain* (*Diogène*, October 1956).

SOYINKA, WOLE: b. 1935 at Abeokuta in the Yoruba country of Western Nigeria. Educated in Ibadan at Government

College and University College, then at Leeds University, where he took English Honours. Taught for a while in London and worked at the Royal Court Theatre, where one of his short plays was produced. In 1960 he returned to Nigeria, where his verse play *A Dance of the Forests* won the *Observer* Competition and was produced for Nigerian Independence in October 1960. Soyinka is actor, musician, and producer as well as poet, and his return to Nigeria has greatly stimulated theatrical life there. In 1965 he joined the English Department at Lagos University. Has published poetry in *Black Orpheus* (of which he is an editor), *Encounter* and elsewhere. He is the first African poet to develop an elegant and good-humoured satirical style, though his recent poetry is darker in tone. *Five Plays* was published by O.U.P. in 1964, and his novel, *The Interpreters*, was published by André Deutsch in 1965. He was arrested by the Federal Government in 1967.

TATI, JEAN-BAPTISTE: b. 1938 at Pointe Noire, Congo. Educated at Pointe Noire, Brazzaville and University of Bordeaux. Has taken a *Licence ès Lettres (Lettres Modernes)*, a *Licence en Italien* and a *Diplome d'études* with a thesis on Benedetto Croce. Is now working on a doctoral thesis on French African poetry. Has completed a first book, *Poèmes de la mer*, which awaits publication. Now returning to Brazzaville to teach at École Normal Supérieure.

U TAM'SI TCHICAYA: b. 1931 at Mpili in the Middle Congo. In 1946 he accompanied his father (then Deputy for Moyen Congo) to France and studied at Orleans and Paris. Has contributed to various French reviews and written many radio features. His poetry exhibits some influence from Césaire, but seems to have a distinctively Congolese passion and intensity. Has published *Le Mauvais Sang*, poems (Caractères, Paris, 1955), *Feu de brousse*, poems (Caractères, 1957), *À Triche-Couer*, poems (Oswald, Paris, 1960), *Épitomé*, poems (Oswald, 1962), and *Le Ventre*, poems (Présence Africaine, 1965). An English translation, *Brush Fire (Feu de Brousse)* was published by Mbari in 1964.

WONODI, OKOGBULE: b. 1936 at Diobu, Eastern Nigeria. Left school at father's death and became a labourer. Later managed to train as a teacher and get to Nsukka University. Took a higher degree at Iowa, where he joined Paul Engle's writers' workshop. His first book of poems, *Ucheke*, was published by Mbari in 1964 under the name of Glory Okugbule Nwanodi, which he has now abandoned.

YAMBO, OUOLOGUEM: No information.

Index

Index of First Lines

265

More About Penguins

Penguin Book News, which appears every month, contains details of all the new books issued by Penguins as they are published. From time to time it is supplemented by *Penguins in Print*, which is a complete list of all books published by Penguins which are in print. (There are nearly three thousand of these.)

A specimen copy of *Penguin Book News* will be sent to you free on request, and you can become a subscriber for the price of the postage – 3s. for a year's issues (including the complete lists). Just write to Dept EP, Penguin Books Ltd, Harmondsworth, Middlesex, enclosing a cheque or postal order, and your name will be added to the mailing list.

Some other books published by Penguins are described on the following pages.

Note: *Penguin Book News* and *Penguins in Print* are not available in the U.S.A. or Canada

The Penguin Book of
South African Verse

Uys Krige and Jack Cope

The Penguin Book of South African Verse is a comprehensive selection which ranges from the end of the nineteenth century to the present day. The English-speaking population of South Africa is hardly more than the population of a medium-sized British or American city like Liverpool or Boston: yet they have given rise to poets in legion, some of whom have found place and acceptance throughout the English-speaking world. In the African languages the transition from the spoken to the written form of poetry is still in active process, beset with difficulties. The group of poems, traditional and contemporary, presented from the main African languages – Sotho, Zulu, Xhosa Bushman, and Hottentot – is not representative, but may be taken as an indication of the wealth that exists. Afrikaans poetry, from its initial impetus after the Anglo-Boer war, has been sustained, enriched, and deepened right up to the present time. Full use is made of the flexibility, vigour, musicality, and idiomatic power of the Afrikaans language.

What may strike the reader in this collection is a preoccupation with violence and death. There is sun, strong colour, and action, but everywhere are the undertones not of pessimism, but of retribution. Suffering, exile and death are familiar to many of these poets born to work under conditions of stress.

African Writing Today

Edited by Ezekiel Mphahlele

A cross-section (in translation, where necessary) of recent
African work in English, French, and Portuguese from the
following countries:
Angola, Cameroon, Congo, Dahomey, Gambia, Ghana,
Guinea, Ivory Coast, Kenya, Moçambique, Nigeria,
Ruanda, Senegal, Sierra Leone, South Africa.

South African Writing Today

Edited by Nadine Gordimer and Lionel Abrahams

This collection of the best recent South African poetry,
prose and drama has been made without regard for
differences of colour or race and shows the strength of
South African writing today. The contributors include Dan
Jacobson, Laurence Lerner, Todd Matshikiza, Ezekiel
Mphahlele, Lewis Nkosi, Alan Paton, William Plomer and
Ronald Segal.

Writing Today

Some reviews of the first four volumes:

'Where it seeks to counter the insularities of our taste
and the unwillingness, in all but a few places, to study
literature comparatively, it is an admirable venture' –
George Steiner in the *New Statesman*

'Penguins deserve a resounding cheer for launching this
splendid new series of paperbacks devoted to contemporary
trends in world writing. If this first quartet is anything
to go by, the venture should prove an invaluable
introduction to anyone wishing to broaden his literary
horizons' – Alan Riddell in the *Daily Telegraph*